the
future of
Australia

LIZ ALLEN is a demographer and social researcher, teaching research methods and researching population dynamics at the ANU Centre for Social Research and Methods. She uses her analytic skills to provide much-needed information about data (for example the census and marriage postal survey) or population dynamics (for example immigration and fertility).

Liz has written numerous pieces for *The Conversation*, scholarly articles in academic journals and contributions to research reports. She was named in the inaugural ABC Top 5 Humanities and Social Sciences academics in Australia 2018. She can be found on social media under the alter ego of Dr Demography.

the
future of
Australia

Demography gets a makeover

Liz Allen

NEWSOUTH

A NewSouth book

Published by
NewSouth Publishing
University of New South Wales Press Ltd
University of New South Wales
Sydney NSW 2052
AUSTRALIA
newsouthpublishing.com

A catalogue record for this book is available from the National Library of Australia

ISBN   9781742236506 (paperback)
        9781742244785 (ebook)
        9781742249285 (ePDF)

Design Josephine Pajor-Markus
Cover design and illustration Design by Committee

Contents

Beyond destiny

The future worries me. It keeps me awake at night. In Australia, as in much of the world, there are now more older people than ever before, and fewer younger people. The very core of who we are as a nation is undergoing major transformation, and exactly what might happen next is uncertain, as proportionally more Australians age out of the workforce and fewer young people fill the void. How will the competing demands and needs of the young versus older people be reconciled, especially when children don't have a say in the nation's democratic processes? How are people of working age – the nation's economic lifeblood – going to fare, when they've been locked out of the housing market, and when increased pressure to balance family and work already has real consequences for their health and wellbeing? And how will government adequately provide for people in their old age if there aren't enough workers contributing personal income tax to fund government coffers? I worry about the Australia my children will inherit – but as a demographer, I also have hope.

Demography is destiny. It's a bold claim, one uttered a little too often without much consideration of what it

1

means. What's more, it's not actually true. Demography is far more important than mere destiny – it's more like a superpower. By tracing connections between a population's past and present, demographers foresee its future. The true wonder of demography, though, is not its ability to predict the future but to *shape* it, by identifying the challenges that lie ahead and harnessing the opportunities. In that sense, demography goes beyond destiny.

The study of demography centres on population and the dynamics of change – births, deaths and migration – asking how and why these dynamics vary across time and place. At the individual level, our very existence can be understood as a result of broader social, cultural and economic forces that brought our parents together. These same forces shape the trajectory of our lives, translating the socioeconomic circumstances into which we are born into advantage and disadvantage – access and opportunities, or a lack of them. Health, education, employment, home ownership and even voting behaviour are just some of the things that demography can help us to understand and explain.

Think of demography like a Choose Your Own Adventure for the nation – the story of who we were, who we are now, and who we will be, as individuals, families and communities. We are where we are today because of the paths we've taken in the past, and now we're confronted with a series of choices. Take me, for example. My life – just like yours – is a case study in demography. Statisticians could have anticipated much of its course based on my family's socioeconomic status and the events I experienced in child-hood. But it wasn't all written in the stars – or rather des-tined by the stats – because in every Choose Your Own Adventure there are multiple paths, with each new fork leading off in a different direction.

I was born seventh of eight children. My mother trained as a teacher at the local convent, and my father worked in the court system, having entered the public ser-vice via an entry exam after high school. My parents were Catholics and followed the preaching of the pope and local priest almost to the letter. Their lives, and therefore my life, were shaped by the taboo against birth control and the desire, widespread among 'good Catholics', for a large family.

They married later than was usual for early-1970s Australia: Mum was 25 and Dad 32. Because they were older when they married, they had saved money and bought a little red-brick house in the same street as my father's entire family – the same street Dad was raised on. Mum and Dad had both been living at home until the day they married, Mum even sharing a room with her sister until a couple of years before. This was normal back then.

Mum was relatively young by today's standards when she had her first child almost a year after their wedding, but at just shy of 26 she was getting on for the time. Despite this 'late' start, my parents went on to have their eight chil-dren over nearly ten years. Us kids were so closely spaced that my sisters and I were regularly mistaken for triplets. Mum was nearly 35 when she had me – a circumstance unheard of at the time in our community in western Sydney – and by the time I got to school, people mistook her for my grandmother.

I grew up on the inland plains of the Hawkesbury River, at the foot of the Blue Mountains. The landscape was beautiful, but the economic circumstances of the average family living there were pretty low. We literally lived on a flood plain, in an area where government housing was concentrated because the land was cheap. It was fertile land, though, good for farming. There was a big Maltese community, and lots of Maltese migrants worked in the agricultural industry, growing vegetables to feed the population of Sydney.

My family survived on a single income – Mum had left her teaching job when she married my father, a very common thing for the early 1970s – but my parents were savers, and the kitchen cupboards were always stocked like we were prepping for the end of the world. Rows of tinned corn, fish, soup, baked beans and spaghetti lined the pantry, alongside cereals and biscuits (not the sweet ones). Everything had its place in the pantry, and there was a steady rotation of use and replacement. There was always food. It wasn't fancy, but it was nourishing.

It was Dad's experience of austerity as a small child during World War II that influenced the way we lived. He was born in 1938, to parents who'd suffered through the Great Depression, and he'd recount stories of growing up during the war while us kids feigned interest. He'd lived near an army rifle range, and as troops marched past their house on the way to shooting practice, Dad and his brothers would give them fresh vegetables they'd grown in the family's yard. Rolling potatoes down to the men dressed in full army kit as they walked past was Dad's favourite thing to do, because the young men would catch the potatoes like cricket balls and toss them in their packs.

Mum was born in 1945, after the war had ended, after my grandfather returned from service in the merchant navy, and she knew about hardship too. Her family lived right on the edge of Sydney, in harsh bushland. Faith was a major part of Mum's life, so much so that she and her siblings would walk or ride their pushbikes three miles on dirt tracks to get to church services, which were held at a migrant camp nearby. (Her parents didn't go, just the kids. Grandad didn't like that they asked parishioners for money.) In those days you had to fast before mass, so Mum was starving for most of Sunday. She told us stories of near fainting from hunger in the summer heat, before they began sneaking cold cooked sausages into church so they could eat on the bike ride home.

My parents' upbringing – the historical times they'd grown up in and the socioeconomic hardships they experienced – shaped them, and it shaped the way they raised us. They passed their beliefs on to us, both consciously and unconsciously, and their traumas, too, through the stories they told us, and through their behaviour towards each other and us kids. Everyone knows that our parents have a profound and lasting impact on the way we live our lives, but a demographer can tell you that we are influenced by everything from our parents' observance of gender norms to the number of children they had.

Dad would leave to catch the train to work before we woke in the morning, and we'd see him briefly at dinner and before bed. Every day he took a packed lunch of one banana and a sandwich wrapped in brown paper. His briefcase always smelled of ageing banana. As time went on for Dad in his job in the courts, he had to do further study or be left behind. He went to university at night, two hours from home, to get a diploma. Mum picked up the slack, and us kids really didn't notice. Dad prepared one meal a week – hamburgers – and would sometimes bake nut-and-date loaves on the weekend for a treat, but his real place was outside, mowing the lawn and such, and Mum's place was inside doing everything else.

Mum was the first to wake in the morning and the last to sleep. Cleaning, cooking, and ordering of the kid-chaos was Mum's thing. The burden of feeding us kids, getting us all to school on time and coordinating after-school activities all fell to her. We always had clean, ironed clothes, too – how she found the time, I'll never know. The effort required was mammoth, but Mum never questioned her role, and neither did we. She was just doing what her mother had done – and she never left the house without a splash of lippy and wearing a pair of stockings, even in the summer.

All this might make it sound as though my child-hood was an easy one, with caring parents, a roof over my head, plenty to eat and all my material needs taken care of, but it was not. I was eight years old when I was sexually abused by a close relative, and a couple of years older when a teacher began abusing me and a group of other girls at my Catholic primary school. In both cases, I was told that as a victim of abuse I was being punished in God's name, and that silence was imperative, as the scandal that would follow if I spoke about it would bring shame on my family. Religion played a big part in the life of our town, and we were closely involved in the church through school and our family's social circle, so I had to keep the abuse a secret. At first I told myself that this was a normal part of growing up. It happened to everyone. It was God's will. But by the time I hit high school, I knew it wasn't normal – no loving god would want this – and it tore me apart. The abuse I suffered was concealed by the very people who should have protected me, because they chose to protect themselves and the perpetrators instead.

The pain was unbearable, and at 13 I attempted suicide. Fortunately I survived, but at the time I was pretty angry about my failure to get even that right. I was placed in a special home for kids who'd experienced trauma. Lumping a whole heap of traumatised young people together isn't such a great way to help them overcome their difficulties, though – you just share the trauma around. I tried to live with my family again afterwards, but it was too difficult, like trying to squeeze a square peg through a round hole, and we all emerged a little more damaged. I never really settled back into family life and just jumped around from place to place, staying in institutions, at refuges and with friends. School was not an option, either. Year 7 was as far as I completed. I tried returning to school in year 8 and again in year 9, but my lack of stable accommodation and the unresolved trauma I was suffering meant mainstream schooling was out of the question.

Strangely, amidst all the bad, I stumbled across one of the best things in my life – my boyfriend. It was love at first sight for me. I remember saying to a friend at the time, 'I will one day have that boy's babies.' What's interesting is that I'd never really thought about being a mother until that point, whereas for women of my mother's generation, the question wasn't *if* a woman would have children, it was *when*.

Mum and Dad finally had enough of me, and eight days after my sixteenth birthday they called the police and had me removed from the family home. They thought being homeless would send me straight, force me to overcome the trauma and move on. Life got really tough, but I survived, keeping my possessions in a garbage bag so I could move about quickly. My little wooden hairbrush, a gift from my sister for my twelfth birthday, was the only thing I had to remind me of home. That little hairbrush lasted as long as it could before it split and fell apart. Symbolic, really.

The hardship and deprivation that you suffer when you're homeless are all consuming. Life's essentials – shelter, food and water – are unpredictable, and the resulting exposure, hunger and thirst are physically and emotionally overwhelming. Not knowing where or when you'll be able to get a clean drink of water causes great stress, and this stress occupies the full capacity of your brain, so much so that thinking about anything else – like getting a job – is totally ridiculous. Being hungry is just as bad, and being unable to bathe not only stops you going to interviews or turning up for work, it also undermines your sense of control over your own body. I can still feel these things deep within, like a physical pain. I longed to be like everyone else, normal. To blend into the crowd and not be noticed for the poor-people clothes I wore, the holey, smelly shoes that never fit. Being homeless didn't just change the way I looked; it drained me of my optimism for life, and I was greeted each day by a sense of hopelessness. I was lucky to find a safe place living with my boyfriend and his family. A family who helped the once-damaged kid to grow.

Soon I was pregnant – and ecstatic. I so longed for a family of my own, a place to belong … unconditionally. I was still just 16, and being a teen parent was bloody hard, but oh-so worth it. I often look back in disbelief that we survived. Don't ever listen to anyone who tells you teen parenthood is a phase of life that one grows out of, by the way. It's not. I will always be a teen mum, no matter my age. It changes you forever. Aside from having very little money and having to rely on welfare or charity, people look at you differently, assuming you're a bad parent and incapable of lovingly raising a child. Teen mums have to work many times harder than other mums just to be seen as competent. Throughout my pregnancy, I was constantly afraid the government would take my child. Booking in to deliver my daughter at the hospital validated my fears. The nurse told me I'd be giving my unborn child up for adoption. I said no, sternly. No one was taking my family from me. Life was a daily battle from then on. Being a minor and having a child is tricky: you don't have full social rights yourself, yet you have to defend those of your child. Your educational and employment opportunities are greatly reduced, and you can't improve your financial position by saving – the money coming in goes straight out again, just to get by from week to week. The emotional and financial stress combine to limit the lifelong possibilities of a teen mum.

I returned to finish school at 18, through Mount Druitt TAFE. It was a hike from home, and I often had to decide between paying the train fare and getting to school or eating for the day. School always won. My partner cared for our daughter while I finished year 10 and then prepared for tertiary study. I was accepted to study applied chemistry at a posh Sydney university – but when I got there, I hated every second of it. And I sucked at it too. I withdrew and got a casual job while I awaited the next semester's intake for a social science degree at Macquarie University. When classes started, I was the odd one out. I wore second-hand clothes I had altered to make them mine and Big W look-alike knock-off shoes. The other students in my classes saw through all this and often laughed at me. Plus, every time I spoke in class I sounded less refined than the rest of them. I spent my time in the library, typing out my assignments, which I'd painstakingly written by hand on the two-hour commute each way to and from the university each day.

I had no friends, and it was lonely. I always struggled to maintain friendships – it's near impossible when your life is in ruins, and between work, study and motherhood, life was too busy anyway. But I was passing my courses, and I was happy. It wasn't until my final year of university that I made a friend. She was kind and smart, and we bonded over our love for demography – seriously we did. I realised then that maybe I was finally normal, because someone normal saw me as their equal and worthy of their friendship – something I desperately wanted.

I survived university and graduated, with my partner and by then two children there to see me get my degree. Then I landed a job in Canberra, and we all packed up and moved to the capital. I've since completed a master's degree and a PhD, juggling kids and work. I've had more children, too – as demographers know, the earlier you start having children, the more children you're likely to have overall – and my partner is still with me. (Bless him.) I never dreamed I'd study so much. But for me, education was my ticket out of a mess, a passport to some sort of freedom … and hope. Something else a demographer could tell you is that there are more employment opportunities for graduates, and that the higher income associated with higher qualifications is also associated with upward social mobility.

I fell into studying demography by accident in my first year as an undergraduate. I had to fill my elective quota for the semester, and the choice was between something called jurisprudence and demography – I had to google both for definitions. Jurisprudence looked boring, and I could barely pronounce it, but demography looked interesting. When classes started, I got hooked. Demography was empowering. It allowed me to understand my life – where I had come from and why things were so bloody hard – and relieved me of the personal blame and shame I'd carried with me for so many years. I finally understood how much harder I had to work than the rest of the students at university, struggling just to tread water while they had all the gear they needed to do fancy synchronised swimming routines. Sure, I couldn't afford to buy textbooks and course readers, and so had to be at every class to take comprehensive notes. But it didn't matter, because demography helped me to see that life was a lottery. Education, health, housing and work opportunities – they all come down to our family's financial circumstances.

I'm still just that poor kid, and my possessions and such are plain, but my demography-by-accident decision serendipitously led me to something incredibly rewarding: I get to help change the world. Even just a little teensy tiny bit. I feel like I have a superpower in what I know about demography. And I want to flick on my cape – and swish it round a bit, because how cool are capes? – and share my passion for demography with you. So, having looked at my own life as a case study, let's get back to why we're here!

At the most basic level, demography is about age and sex. Sex is important because a surplus of one sex or the other makes a population's future terribly uncertain. And age is important because it determines the opportunities and challenges a population faces. A young population – for example, one in which half the population is aged under 20 – benefits from what is known as the 'demographic dividend', as a large chunk of the total population enters the workforce within a short period of time. Relatively more people in the workforce means an income tax windfall for government. Economic development is often rapid in such societies, helping to lift individuals, families and entire communities out of poverty. An older population, on the other hand – for example, one with more than half the population aged 50 and over – faces demographic challenges, because it has substantially more people no longer working yet requiring support.

In much of the world, discussions of population now centre around below-replacement fertility and ageing. Think more older people and fewer kids. We're living longer than ever before, but we're having too few babies to ensure steady generational churn. That poses a problem: the pool of government finances is shrinking relative to need. At the same time, natural resources are being placed under increasing pressure, a problem only exacerbated by climate change. Shrinking resources mean difficult decisions: national budgets have to take into account a whole range of urgent yet competing priorities. Wealth inequality also poses a significant challenge in many countries, and this is definitely the case in Australia, where economic disparities between older Australians and younger people starting out in life spell even greater uncertainty for our nation's future prosperity.

Economically advanced countries are undeniably in the midst of unprecedented transformation – but with this transformation come potential opportunities. The need to cope with climate change and redress wealth inequality grants a social licence for wider change. This is an opportunity for demographers, too: rather than using our knowledge of the past and present to anticipate one future, we can help to identify many possible futures, and the paths towards them. Demography can take centre stage as a planning tool. Unfortunately, though, politicians and powerbrokers have long preferred to use demography as a political tool, seeking to unite or divide societies for their own ends. The media plays right into their game, fanning the flames through sensational, attention-grabbing headlines that politicians both feed and react to. One minute it's declining populations and too many older people they're worried about; the next it's being inundated by swarming migrants and refugees.

Migration is, of course, a common theme in discussions of population. Throughout Australia's history, overseas migration has featured prominently in public debate, sometimes seen as a positive, sometimes as a negative, but never far from the agenda. The trouble is that media headlines and political catchphrases all too often misrepresent the facts. In the extreme, political players exploit fears relying on nothing but anecdote: Australia is overpopulated, they say, and immigrants are stealing locals' jobs, robbing young people of their future. Resources are too scarce, they say, to support a larger population. I'll be taking on this outdated and now debunked idea of 'carrying capacity' later, asking why it is still so influential.

No matter your stance on any of these questions, there's no denying the fundamental nature of the transformation we're going through. But unprecedented change doesn't have to be a crisis. The stakes in this Choose Your Own Adventure story are high, but we do have options. We're not inevitably bound for doom and dystopia. There are desirable futures on the horizon, but to reach them will take work – preparedness, planning, responsiveness – and we have to act now. We have to work together, too, because this story belongs to us all – a gift bestowed on us by the past, to be built on today, for the benefit of the future.

The decisions we face demand a sensible and considered point of view, and that's where demography comes in, with its data-driven approach and insistence on evidence. In this book I'll give you an overview of significant demographic milestones in Australia's history, establishing where we've come from and where we stand today, before outlining the bounds of what lies ahead. While we can never be exactly sure how things will play out, we can predict likely outcomes, and make strategic decisions about the future on that basis. My perspective on demography is of course framed by my own personal circumstances, but I hope as you read this book that you'll recognise yourself in it, too. I want you to start thinking about your own story, and asking yourself questions:

How has your life has been shaped by demography?
How does your story fit into the larger story of your
family, your community, your nation – the story of us?
And what is it that *you* want for the future of us?

PART 1

The story of us

CHAPTER 1

How we got here:
The peopling of Australia

The circle of life, from birth to death, is a story as old as time itself. This might sound like the overture to a Disney film, complete with princes, princesses, music and magic, but the story of us is far from a fairytale. There is no magic ... but I promise wonder.

Around a hundred billion people have so far been born, lived and died on earth. Those of us alive today represent only a small fraction of that total number. The story of today's world starts with all those billions of people who came before us – generation after generation, each contributing their own chapter.[1] It's the story of all the people who've gone before us that has shaped the modern world. As a demographer, it's my job to help others read that story – a story we're all characters in – and to figure out what might be in store for us next. Demographers aren't like the prophets or fortune tellers of old, though – we're scientists, and our reading of the past and expectations of the future are based on evidence. We have our own lingo, which might seem arcane at first, but if you read on you'll soon be talking demographics and data sets like a pro. But let's take a look at the basics first, before we get too technical. Get ready. Demography will forever shift your world view.

No, I can't tell you the meaning of life. And, no, I can't answer your questions about the origins of the human species. But what I can do, as a demographer, is to explain the here and now by looking back at the past – at the pathways travelled and the lives lived. Standing in the present, with the past holding us firm against the headwinds of the future, demography provides a map, helping us to anticipate what's ahead and plot the path we desire. While I won't be answering any existential questions, I can offer you the world … the past, present and future.

Population dynamics: A primer

Deaths and taxes. The two certainties in life, right? Well, forget what you think you know: for demographers the three certainties are birth, death and migration, or, as we like to call them, fertility, mortality and migration. (Spoiler alert: taxes are still pretty important – but we'll discuss that later.) When demographers talk about the 'dynamics of population', we're typically referring to these three major life events. The demographic composition of a population can be understood by measuring the number and rate of births and deaths, and the flow of people in and out of a specific place.

Measuring births might sound straightforward, but it's not. It's easy to count what we refer to in crude demographic speak as 'live births', but a demographer's interest in births extends far beyond a simple tally of babies born. We want to understand births within their social context, and there are many variables to take into account. For a start, the lead-up to pregnancy, planned or unplanned, involves a complex set of negotiations, not always entered into by willing participants. Women have different reproductive rights in different societies, and varying levels of bodily autonomy. Wealth, health and status all play a role in partnering, in the initial decision to have a baby, and in decisions about family size. All of this information helps us to understand not only how individuals come to be born, but how they might live.

Similarly, death isn't just a one-time event for demographers – there's a lifetime of lead-up. Even before conception, our deaths have to some extent been mapped out for us by the genes we've inherited from our parents. Whether we're prone to addiction, heart disease or cancer, it's all there in our DNA. But it's not just about nature; it's also about nurture. The influence of caregivers is important, as is the environment in which we are raised. Demographers often seek to understand death in terms of the two M's: morbidity and mortality. Morbidity refers to illness and disability, and the impact they have on individuals and populations. Death and illness are reduced to statistics in demography – quantified as probability or risk, in the form of age-specific rates of disease and death, and of course average life expectancy. But what you should know is that there is only probability, never certainty, because there are always exceptions to the rule. Take lung cancer, for example. Some non-smokers will die of lung cancer, while some heavy smokers might live to 112, despite what the statistics tell us to expect.

One thing is certain, though: the average lifetime trajectory towards death is faster for someone in poorer health, and poverty limits access to health services, with far-reaching results. Poor dental care, for example, is linked to the development of heart disease in later life, but the cost of fixing a broken tooth may seem prohibitive to someone on a low income, meaning that it goes untreated. Think of life as climbing a staircase. An individual born to healthy, wealthy parents living in a wealthy area starts life on a considerably higher step than, say, someone who is born to parents suffering ill health and living in a socioeconomically disadvantaged area. Over the course of their lives, the person born into relative advantage will be offered far more opportunities and climb the staircase of success at a much faster rate than the person born into disadvantage. Unfortunately, the position we're born into is the one we typically remain in – there's very little social mobility the world over.[2] Hard work matters little for a person born poor, because socioeconomic status constrains our options. The area we live in, the schools we attend, our educational attainments and the type of job we do – all come down to the relative wealth of our parents.

Even when death comes suddenly, it doesn't come out of nowhere – it's also a matter of probability. Poverty, smoking, alcohol, drug use, risky driving, lack of education, poor diet, infectious diseases, insufficient vaccination, poor working conditions and unsafe sex are just some of the risk factors associated with an early death. In fact, while life expectancy in Australia today is 81 for men and 85 for women,[3] experts say it should be around 122 years.[4] The fact that it isn't comes down to the environment in which we grow up and the way we live our lives.

At the end of the day – or rather the end of our lives – our most important bodily soft bits fail us. The elixir of life lies in countering the degeneration of our mere mortalness. Until the day science can solve this problem (perhaps by sticking the ageing brain in a bottle for preservation), our lives and thus our deaths are constrained by the suite of risk factors determining health and longevity. Sadly, risk is highly correlated with socioeconomic status.

It's rare we live in the same house, in the same town, from birth to death. We move around, though of course we might return. Our movements reflect the opportunities we're given, which are shaped by our age, interests and needs: education and training, work, travel, relationships. Just as birth and death are facts of life, migration has always been and will always be a part of human life. Exploration and trade, sparked by human interest and ingenuity, were among the main motivators of early migration. Throughout history, vast numbers of people have moved across borders, fleeing persecution in conflict-ravaged countries or seeking a safe place to establish roots.

Across the world, migration has been, and remains, a gift for those who live alongside migrants, as much as for the migrants themselves. People who migrate are typically adventurous and entrepreneurial; they're effective risk-takers. The personality traits associated with moving away from family and cultural familiarity to seek out opportunities are the same necessary for making innovations in business. Greater diversity in experiences also position migrants to be more open to the global economy. This is true even when they are forced by circumstance to migrate – which is often the case. Large-scale movements of people haven't always been, nor are they now, peaceful. The practice of forced movement is seen in Australia's own history, with First Nations peoples. Entire populations were rounded up and pushed into settlements away from cultural homelands. A history still visible in its effect on modern times.

Indigenous Australia

No attempt to describe the demography of the Australian continent from the earliest times could ever do it justice. All I can offer here is a mere glimpse of the lives of its founding peoples, the ancestors of Indigenous Australians and Torres Strait Islanders, from the point of view of a non-Indigenous researcher working with an incomplete and partial record – but even so, it's an extraordinary story.

The very existence of First Nations peoples in Australia is a powerful tale of human wonder and the desire to explore. (I promised wonder, didn't I?) At the time of the first major human migration to what we now know as Australia, both Tasmania and New Guinea were still joined to the Australian mainland, forming a landmass that scientists refer to as 'Sahul'. This migration took place an estimated 65 000 years ago, but current scholarship suggests it could be much greater than this.[5] The peopling of Sahul was by no means an accident or chance event. Without the benefit of physical maps or charts (or GPS devices, for the kids among us), the ancestors of the First Nations Australians migrated in large groups over land and across seas from the north. These were sophisticated expeditions requiring calculated planning and technological nous.[6]

The story of the peopling of Sahul isn't like the story of Adam and Eve and their descendants populating the earth, or Noah surviving the flood in his ark – more myth or legend than history. It has much more in common with the story of the first British colonists to travel to Australia. In movement but not dispossession. With migration to Australia and the short-term survival and eventual successful establishment of a new population, there were complex logistical exercises involving long-term planning – not just a one-off voyage of a handful of people, or a journey undertaken in a single, biblically proportioned vessel.

Evidence points to a journey of at least 1300 people, in watercraft designed to withstand the brutality of the open waters between what is now known as Indonesia and Australia.[7] Moving between island chains required a level of organisation and logistical planning beyond the imagination. It's extraordinary to think about what this must have involved: crafting vessels by hand from hollowed-out trees, making them watertight, and finding a place on board for all the tools, materials and resources they'd need to survive in the new land.

Non-Indigenous Australians have long failed to recognise that the demographic story of First Nations Australians is one of innovation, ingenuity and sophistication. Establishing themselves in their new home would have been like creating a new world. Observations of the landscape and environment through scientific data collection to inform where to live and how to hunt are still relied upon. Over time, as they gradually moved across the Sahul landmass, new kinship groups developed, forming a tightly woven net of peoples and population groups, each with their own territory, which they came to know intimately, and their own unique culture and language.

They developed deep cultural and spiritual connections to the land, seeing themselves as its custodians. They moved within their own country in accordance with the seasons – a sophisticated form of environmental management – and to observe cultural rituals, such as those surrounding births and deaths. Reciprocal relationships persisted among neighbouring clans and mobs, who met for celebrations, negotiations and trade, and to facilitate information sharing about relevant news and observations. Coastal communities also maintained strong trade networks with Australia's nearest neighbours, especially to the north, following the split of the mainland that broke up Sahul.

Prior to British colonisation, the Indigenous population was healthy, and thriving. With natural borders of vast oceans and rich inland waterways, they were not threatened by epidemics in the way that European populations so often were. When they killed animals for their meat, nothing was wasted; the skins, fur, sinew and bones were used to make weaponry and clothing. It was a system sustainable over the long term: their law mandated respect for the land and its non-human inhabitants.

Life prior to colonisation was not without its risks. Childbirth was risky for both mother and baby, but not significantly riskier than it would have been in any other country at the time. Mothers gave birth under the care of female elders, who gave them much the same kind of support that a midwife would have provided in other cultures, including most European cultures, at that time. After birth itself, infancy was one of the riskiest periods in a person's life. In general, with independence and maturation, child health peaks, and the risk of death abates until adolescence. In the lead-up to early adulthood, risk of death increased again, and peaked at its highest across the life course, owing to the activities in which individuals were engaged (like hunting, getting into physical confrontations, and just generally mucking around). These patterns of mortality are still observed in present populations. High mortality and life expectancy around the forties were likely due to health risks associated with the limited medical knowledge of the time. Yet clean water, food preparation and waste management, and the seasonal migratory nature of living, resulted in the reduction of environmental contamination that would have threatened health. The mortality rate would not have been all that different to that experienced by British people at home in Britain.

It remains a common, insidious myth that First Nations Australians did not use the land and its resources in a way that visitors from the outside world, and later the British invaders, could recognise as such. It is true that Europeans grossly underestimated the sophistication of Indigenous Australian cultures. It is also true that such ethnocentric prejudices underpinned the self-serving assertion that Australia was terra nullius – land belonging to nobody. It is not true, however, that British colonisers saw no evidence of settled populations, active land management or agricultural activity when they arrived in Australia.

There is clear evidence that First Nations Australians actively managed the land they lived on.[8] This management was vital not only to the protection and preservation of the land but also to its ability to sustain them. The ecological techniques they used were mastered over millennia and passed down through the generations, ensuring their continued survival. Firestick farming is perhaps one of the best known of these techniques: fires were strategically lit to clear away dead undergrowth, encouraging new grass to grow, which attracted kangaroos, wallabies and other grazing animals, making them easier to corral and kill, guaranteeing a reliable and predictable source of protein that could then be prepared for eating and sharing.[9] The immense importance of this particular land management strategy is clear today: the cessation of careful and coordinated firestick farming has resulted in the devastation of bushfires plaguing life and country.

The damming of waterways and construction of fishing traps to catch aquatic animals for food also has a long history among First Nations peoples: evidence of this kind of aquaculture goes back well over 6000 years. There was no indiscriminate casting of massive nets on their watch, but rather cautious monitoring and farming.[10] The Budj Bim eel traps in south-western Victoria near Port Fairy provide a phenomenal example: water from Darlot Creek was channelled into the surrounding wetlands, trapping the eels in a series of weirs, ensuring a year-round supply that could be harvested as they matured.[11] There is emerging evidence that the Gunditjmara, the First Nations peoples of the region, didn't just farm eel, but also smoked the meat as a way of preserving it, allowing them to trade it with other communities. Heather Builth has proven the construction of permanent stone dwellings at Budj Bim in her investigations using computerised topographical mapping.[12] While seasonal movement of the First Nations peoples of this region may well have continued after the construction of fixed dwellings, it's clear there were firm connections to fixed sites, and sufficient resources, in this particular case, to sustain year-round living.

Colonisers destroyed parts of the Budj Bim aquaculture system around the mid-1800s, draining the streams of water,[13] and in doing so destroyed evidence of the economic activity of First Nations peoples in the region. This destruction no doubt aided in the construction of the narrative of *terra nullius* falsely perpetuated by the colonisers, who said they saw no tilling of the land, no economic activity, no fixed structures. Despite these attempts at destruction, the culture and livelihoods of the First Nations peoples of the region, the Budj Bim aquaculture system survives to this day, testament to the ingenuity and cultural sophistication of the region's first occupants.

Aquaculture and firestick farming are just two examples of how the First Nations peoples of Australia more than merely lived with the harsh Australian conditions. They are part of a larger pattern of clear and undeniable proof that Australian landscapes were meticulously managed, drawing on sophisticated knowledge of the natural environment, to supply clans with nutritious diets over many millennia, right across the vast landmass of Australia.

Much of the mainstream history of Australia fails to recognise the sophisticated economic activities of First Nations peoples. Trade with neighbouring countries is just one part of the story. Relationships were established and maintained between First Nations peoples in northern Australia and Indonesian seafarers to trade seafood in exchange for items including fabric, rice, tobacco and weaponry.[14] In many history books, though, the economic history of Australia seems to commence upon European colonisation. Everything that happened before colonisation is viewed through a white European ethnocentric lens of knowledge and being. Relying on the interpretation of complex intricacies of culture and practice by outsiders looking only superficially in hides realties and truth. We tend to only see what we know, and in doing so look for evidence of others holding our own values and norms. The first step to understanding the complete economic history of Australia, as the work by economist Boyd Hunter suggests, is to understand the population, its dynamics and geographic distribution. Hunter's thesis when it comes to acknowledging and compiling Australia's complete economic history is to capture oral storytelling from First Nations peoples for enduring preservation.[15] As far as the economic history of Australia is concerned, for many, if it hasn't been documented in the written form, and often specifically in English, then it didn't happen. This simplistic whitewashing belies the richness of the Australian story, robbing the First Nations peoples of their past by writing off any economic activities, and stealing the potential of the future by overlooking opportunities for the continuance of rich and diverse practices.

Drawing on earlier work by archeologist John Mulvaney (the so-called father of the discipline in Australian) and economic historian Noel Butlin, and the use of somewhat disputed mapping of Aboriginal clans and languages, Boyd Hunter and medical scientist John Carmody[16] sought to estimate the total First Nations population of mainland Australia prior to colonisation, and to examine the initial impact and continuing effect of the colonisers on the Indigenous population. Most recent estimates by Hunter and Carmody place the total population before colonisation at around 800 000 peoples, but it might have been anywhere between 500 000 and 1.2 million.[17] Regardless of its size, though, this population was healthy. Colonisation brought with it disease and death. Chickenpox and smallpox were introduced to the Australian continent and spread faster than colonial frontiers. Germs spread like deadly invisible frontiers. A population and people enjoying remarkably good health were infected, perhaps even deliberately so, with diseases that resulted in vast numbers of deaths. In fact, Hunter and Carmody estimate that the First Nations population on mainland Australia fell by nearly 40 per cent, or around 300 000 people, within the first few years of colonisation.

Together, disease, frontier fighting and deliberate killings took an enormous toll on First Nations Australians, and as the population of colonists increased, the population of First Nations peoples dropped significantly. Within around 50 years, the colonist population exceeded the Indigenous population. This was not due to a sudden influx of colonists, but rather steady colonisation alongside enormous loss of life among the First Nations peoples.

European colonists came to Australia with preconceived ideas about First Nations peoples in Australia. These preconceptions had a fatal influence on their interactions with First Nations peoples they came into contact with. Colonists approached Indigenous people with contempt, in the belief they were inferior, whereas Indigenous people interacted in good faith. The fatal preconceived ideas about the level of sophistication and civility of First Nations peoples is still reflected in contemporary discourse. First Nations peoples are often depicted in mainstream media as inferior to white Australians of European descent. The belief of inferiority results in actions by government and community that further disempower First Nations peoples because Indigenous people are treated like infants needing parenting.

Colonisers failed to see – or at least to acknowledge – the sophisticated social, cultural, legal, economic and agricultural activity going on all around them, because it looked so different to what they were accustomed to.[18] In doing so, the colonisers overlooked – wilfully or otherwise – the custodianship of First Nations peoples over their lands, and the complex social structures that had allowed them to survive in this landscape for thousands of years.

Colonisers began to exert control over First Nations peoples not long after the arrival of the British fleet. The control they sought was all encompassing – taking in everything from physical, social and civic liberties to education and employment, marriage and childbearing – and it was to have long-term, lasting impacts, still evident today. This control was genocidal in its intent.

In the early 1900s, the stolen generations of government-enacted removal of Indigenous children from their families began. First Nations children whose skin was pale enough for assimilation into white Australian society were snatched from their families and lands and placed with strangers. Fair, blue-eyed, blond-haired children were particularly singled out.[19] First Nations children were also removed and placed in group homes, denied the love and care of relatives – all in the name of assimilation, based on the now debunked pseudoscience of eugenics. Eugenics heavily informed the British colonist's approach to Indigenous peoples in Australia. The British believed they could 'breed out' what they believed to be the inferiority of the Indigenous race.

Describing her family's experiences as members of the stolen generations, academic Aileen Marwung Walsh explains the intergenerational trauma caused by this horrific eugenic policy and its lasting impacts. Walsh's mother was forcibly taken from her family and, as a result of this traumatic experience, went on to develop alcohol dependency and psychiatric difficulties in her adult life – which led to Walsh herself being sent to a children's home. Walsh recounts her immense fear, and the measures she took to protect herself:

> There was the constant worry that I was going to be interfered with. The bed had this revolting vinyl cover that you were meant to fold back at night. But I didn't. I kept that vinyl cover over me, even though it made me sweat like a pig and it went mouldy on the underside, but I felt a bit safer.[20]

Walsh recounts a story of bravery and overcoming, one that highlights her love of country, of her home among the spinifex, where she knew she walked on First Nations land. But despite this abiding connection to country, Walsh's life, and her family's life, would never be the same again:

A lot of my childhood was spent moving around. At the time I didn't mind too much, but my sisters hated it. The years of the Stolen Generations in Australia have had profound effects on Aboriginal families such as mine. Though I didn't spend a long stretch of time in a children's home, the memory of it is etched indelibly on my mind. And growing up feeling unloved is a terrible feeling.[21]

Dispossession of First Nations peoples from ancestral lands caused at best disruption and at worst complete disconnection from the lands, places and kinship ties that are the spiritual embodiment of identity.[22] It is hard not to see such deleterious policies of dispossession, control and the removal of children from their families as wilful acts intended to undermine and destroy a strong and sophisticated civilisation, or to consider them anything but genocide.

The foundation of First Nations societies was, and remains, families. Families in a richer and more sophisticated sense than just mum, dad and siblings. Families are comprised of clan groups – extended families in the non-Indigenous sense – of relatives responsible for nurturing the physical and cultural wellbeing of individuals. Through disease, displacement and killings, clan groups with deep and long-lasting connections to the Australian continent were severely disrupted, and in some cases largely wiped out. Languages and cultures were attacked and destroyed. But First Nations Australians endure

as proud and tenacious peoples, despite the colonists'
attempts to eradicate them.

Population transformations

Innumerable events throughout history have helped
shape the population of Australia, so I can only pause long
enough to look at the most momentous milestones here –
those which have had an enduring effect on the Australian
population and way of life.

The history of First Nations peoples in Australia makes
it very clear the country is merely one part of the world
population. Australia was originally populated by significant movements of people from other parts of the globe.
But the written history of Australia excludes First Nations
peoples from the narrative describing the building of the
nation. This is in part due to the fact that First Nations
Australians were not included in official counts of the
population, and partly because Indigenous peoples were
excluded from much of the so-called mainstream social
and economic activity. Movement, marriage and civic participation generally remained tightly controlled until the
1970s, even into the 1980s, and arguably later. Wage theft,
lack of voting rights, and the forced removal of children
perpetuated the notion that Indigenous Australians were
fringe dwellers: a segregation of sorts. The maltreatment
of and malevolence toward Indigenous Australians made it
near impossible for First Nations peoples to take equal part
in so-called mainstream society.

Following colonisation, the British government focused its efforts on populating the vast landmass of Australia with free settlers from Britain. The creation of a white Australia was the goal – building the 'right' kind of population as a means to secure the territory for Britain. The initial wave of colonists comprised military personnel and convicts sent from what was often referred to as the 'mother country'. Supplying a suitable stock of British women to even the balance of the sexes in the male-dominated colony was a particular concern; hooliganism, alcohol use and sexually transmitted diseases were rife among the colonisers, and it was thought that the presence of 'decent' women would help keep the soldiers and free men in line by offering comfort and support, and later provide the colony with children. In 1796, the first year that such information was officially collected, it was estimated that there were around three men per woman in the colony.[23] At the time of colonisation, there would have likely been a much greater sex disparity. That disparity increased between 1796 and the eventual turning point in 1803, when it started to go down. A roughly equal distribution of the sexes, like that seen in most populations, was not reached until a decade into the 20th century. This was short-lived, however: when men went to fight in World War I, women remained to fight from home and outnumbered men until 1919.

Demand for fertile farming land across the Sydney area saw more and more First Nations territory forcibly seized to make way for colonial agriculture. Trees were cleared, wildlife indiscriminately slaughtered and sacred sites violated. The lives of First Nations peoples were treated with malice, many losing their lives or harmed, all in the name of the colony. Mass burial sites and the physical scars of indiscriminate land clearing still mark the Australian landscape today.

This control was also demonstrated in the immigration of people to Australia. Prior to Federation, migrants came to Australia from all over the world to try their luck on what was considered a new frontier. The gold-rush period of Australian history offers considerable insight into the way the British colonisers regarded people of different races. There was frequent conflict between British people and First Nations peoples, and also between the British and other non-British immigrants. First Nations Australians however have a long history of peaceful exchange and experience with other visitors, and Chinese people in particular, which even predates colonisation.[24]

At the time of national federation, in 1901, fertility rates were as high as an average of eight children per woman.[25] This was due to high mortality and uncontrolled fertility. There was also a paternalistic push for procreation among those in the colony. Securing a nation through population growth has been a practice promoted throughout history, so it's no surprise that the colonising peoples sought to build up their numbers.

Immigration, and the characteristics of migrants, were a major issue at the time of Federation. One of the new federal government's first acts was to effectively close the borders, and to limit immigration, especially from Asian countries. Prior to Federation, policies were already in place in most states to control Asian migration. The White Australia policy, in the form of the Immigration Restriction Act of 1901, was designed to limit the immigration of Asian- and African-born people in particular. Migrants could be forced to take a language dictation test, in any European language – not necessarily English – and denied entry if they failed it.[26] The point was to exclude non-Europeans from Australia. The government of the day couldn't bring themselves to realise anything other than a pro-European dream of what Australia might be.

Throughout the subsequent decades, including the Great Depression and the two world wars that followed, the theme of border protection remained a constant in Australian political rhetoric. Australia was not immune to the global instability of this period. To cope with the economic pressures of the time, a minimum male wage was enacted, sufficient to support a wife and three children.[27] The goal was to ensure all families had adequate income by limiting jobs to one per family. The male breadwinner model was somewhat state endorsed because of the stigma associated with women being in paid work over their male partners, and the financial penalty of their wages being half that of men's. In practice, this resulted in women having to leave paid employment the moment they married or had a child. The notion of work, and access to paid work, were well and truly gendered during this period. This social norm endured long after any economic need, as late as the 1980s, especially for women in government jobs, and in certain occupations, such as teaching.

Over roughly the same period – from Federation to around the 1970s – as modes of production changed, children's economic contribution to their families changed too. They were increasingly seen not as economic assets but as individuals with rights of their own. Governments in Australia, starting with New South Wales, began to provide free schooling and family payments to help lighten the economic load of raising children.

Early child endowment payments further entrenched the male breadwinner model of the Australian family. Nuclear families with stay-at-home mums were those to benefit most, meaning white, non-Indigenous Australians became the most socially desirable family construct. Today's family tax benefits system still promotes and perpetuates this model, that the ideal family is one with a stay-at-home parent, which largely reflects the male 'head' of the family going out to work and the mother staying at home to care for kids.

World War II marked a major crossroads for Australia and dawned the golden age of economic prosperity following years of austerity. The beginning of the end of the White Australia policy was forced by postwar nation building and global influences. A push to 'populate or perish' became the flavour of the immediate postwar period, affecting population dynamics well into the 1960s. The fear driving this policy was that Australia didn't have the numbers to protect itself from any external (or internal) threat. Two world wars had frightened the nation into shifting away from its exclusionary stance out of sheer necessity. Australia also found itself in a precarious financial position, having experienced hard economic times since World War I. Increased population had the added benefit of strengthening the nation's financial position. Among the postwar strategies of nation building were population growth targets: one per cent from net overseas migration, and one per cent from natural increase.[28] Assisted migration was offered to the British, and the term 'ten-pound Pom' entered Australia's vernacular. But the potential supply of British migrants was insufficient to meet Australia's growth targets, and so Australia opened immigration to southern and eastern Europeans. Curiously, this measure was introduced at a time when anti-foreigner sentiment among the Australian public was growing.[29]

The need to rehome millions of displaced people worldwide in the aftermath of World War II was a monumental shift for Australian immigration. Motivated largely by the need for more people to contribute to the labour market, an Australian parliamentarian travelled to Europe searching for suitable migrants, at the request of Labor Prime Minister Ben Chifley. What eventuated was an initial agreement with the International Refugee Organization to accept 4000 displaced people from European refugee camps.[30] Australia would go on to accept over 170000 displaced people from Europe.[31] The priority was for people most like Britons – Europeans from the north-western parts of Europe – but a lack of interest meant Australia broadened the net to include people from south-western Europe and eastern Europe, changing the face of Australia forever. Food, language and religion diversified in Australia, setting the scene for services like the Special Broadcasting Service, which have become a feature of contemporary multicultural society.

Infrastructure was a central element of postwar nation building, and the new flows of migrants were set to work in areas and employment the local population was uninterested in.[32] A mandatory period of employment (two years) for such work was enforced for migrants to stay permanently in Australia. Once the mandatory period of attachment was over, migrants were free to find other employment and move elsewhere within Australia. The Snowy Mountains Hydro-Electric Scheme, a decades-long major engineering project, became synonymous with postwar immigration due to the migrant workforce that built it.

The golden age of economic development in Australia following World War II until the 1970s included periods of near full employment and embodied a scientific enlightenment where innovation and developments were being made and experienced in homes across the nation.[33] Australians were witness to scientific improvements: think the dawn of television. Australia was like a go-getting teenager with an attitude immune to anything bad. With this go-getting attitude came a generation of people who would change Australia, and contemporary society is still benefiting (and suffering). This generation would go on to see themselves as pioneers of a new Australia, especially in race relations. Alongside this, with each wave of differing migrant source countries the notion of who was acceptably white enough for Australia morphed each time a group of people more different then the last entered the shores.[34]

Immigration injected a refreshed youthful dynamic to the nation and with it pressures on families. Women had no reliable way to control their fertility and the postwar 'populate or perish' regime had an adverse impact on them. Women were pressured to have children and seen as deviant or selfish if they were unwed, childless or chose not to have children. It would be decades until the oral contraception pill became available in Australia – but when it did, the result was nothing short of transformative for women and society generally.[35] In 1961, Australian women finally gained access to the oral contraceptive pill; then, in 1972, the Whitlam Labor government subsidised oral contraceptives via the national pharmaceutical benefits scheme, making them more accessible. But the arrival of reliable birth control further fuelled the debate about whether unmarried women should have access, and wider arguments about abortion and a woman's control over her body.

The introduction of no-fault divorce marked another seismic shift in society, also introduced by the Whitlam government. In 1975, no longer did couples seeking a divorce need proof of fault. Private investigators rummaging through garbage for evidence of infidelity or inappropriate behaviour became a thing of the past. Prior to no-fault divorce, the statistical reporting of marital separation was included alongside convictions for things like murder. Divorce was viewed almost as a criminal act, and for divorces to be granted, a justifiable reason must have been shown. Data from the early 1950s shows that the reasons given for divorce included impotency, imprisonment of a spouse, insanity, non-consummation, bigamy, adultery and drunkenness.[36]

No-fault divorce gave married individuals, especially women, greater control over their lives. This was a turning point that would eventually lead to the increasing social acceptance and official recognition of many non-traditional relationships, such as de facto and same-sex partnerships.

The Australian Institute of Family Studies was established in 1980 to track the impact of no-fault divorce, and the Child Support Agency was established eight years later to ensure children were adequately provided for by parents.

Together, the introduction of the oral contraceptive pill and no-fault divorce sent a clear signal that women's rights were also central to the nation's rights. Following these monumental introductions came delayed childbearing, child-free families and diverse family structures: in other words, control over one's family circumstances. Individual choice was no longer subordinate to social groupthink. A corollary was an increase in female participation in education – both in the completion of high school and the attainment of post-school qualifications – and in paid employment.

Gender equality increased at a glacial pace, while never reaching parity. With the 21st century came a refocus on immigration, shifting from the population dynamic of fertility in a dramatic way.

Concerns over border protection came to a head again in 2001 under Liberal Prime Minister John Howard,[37] when the MV *Tampa,* a Norwegian freighter carrying rescued asylum seekers, entered Australian waters. Following a great deal of political manoeuvring, misinformation and scaremongering, the Tampa affair resulted in even stricter border protection. The Howard government excised several external territories from the Australian migration zone, to prevent asylum seekers from getting to Australian land for processing of their refugee status. From that point on, asylum seekers coming across the seas looking for protection in Australia were sent to offshore processing centres. The September 11 terrorist attacks in the United States came soon after Tampa, shocking Australia. Howard used the Tampa affair and the events of September 11 to carefully craft a threat of terrorism in Australia – a threat of asylum seekers coming to Australia to cause havoc, and undermine everything Australians had worked hard to create.

Under subsequent governments, both Labor and Coalition, asylum seekers have faced ever-tighter restrictions. They are interned in camps, both onshore and offshore, and in neighbouring countries, and held, indefinitely in some cases, in hellish conditions.

Echoing the rhetoric that accompanied the implementation of the White Australia policy, Howard uttered the words: 'We will decide who comes to this country and the circumstances in which they come.' And so Australia came full circle, frightened, as it had been nearly a century before, by the thought of the unknown other arriving on Australian shores. Howard implanted, exaggerated and promoted a fear of terrorism into the Australian way of life. The government encouraged Australians to see Muslim people as a threat – to our national security, to our way of life – and that over-inflated threat still lingers today, nearly twenty years later.

Enduring white Australia

The White Australia policy officially came to an end in the 1970s under the Whitlam government, with the introduction of the Racial Discrimination Act of 1975, but the idea of a 'White Australia' didn't just go away. Over the years, teachings in schools, conversations over the dinner table, experiences in the workplace and government initiatives had all contributed to an indoctrination of sorts, creating a White Australia mentality that endures to the present day. Generations still alive today were raised with this mentality, and the way in which subsequent generations have been influenced by their parents, grandparents and great-grandparents cannot be underestimated. Taking federal parliament as an example, it is obvious that a significant proportion of our elected officials grew up while the White Australia policy was still in force. Even younger parliamentarians, born post 1975, will inevitably have had some exposure to the ideas that underpinned it, through their interaction with family members, for example, or their teachers at school.

Remnants of the White Australia policy remain omni-present, forming the foundation of national race-based identity. Regardless of the fact Australia has been decades without the discriminatory White Australia policy, the visual and aural otherness of migrants potentially leads to a distinction between 'us' and 'them'. White (European) Australia versus any deviation from the average.

As you would imagine, First Nations Australians did not, and do not, fit comfortably within this concept of White Australia. Indigenous Australians were (and are) treated as the other in their own lands, even though First Nations peoples were literally here first and had tamed the vast continent before whitefellas came to claim something that they had no right to.

First Nations Australians were harshly marginalised in the new Australia through maltreatment and exclusion, from federation until the hard-fought agitation and calls for recognition began to be answered by government.

In the mid-1960s, Oodgeroo Noonuccal, then known publicly as Kath Walker, published a poem called 'The Dawn Is at Hand', about her hope for much-needed change and an end to First Nations peoples being pushed to the margins.[37]

Noonuccal's poem was a call to action for Indige-nous Australians to take their rightful place in society as first peoples, a birthright denied for so long. The anguish of being refused justice, barred from full participation in society, and the racism suffered at the hands of white Australians is palpable throughout the seven stanzas. The call to action speaks of the opportunities on the horizon, of being 'fringe-dwellers no more', and oozes a hope for the future, while recognising the pain of the past and present. Despite the horrors perpetrated against First Nations peoples, no reprisals are suggested. Through great bravery, Noonuccal signals the dawn of the future in the form of mateship, freedom and equality.

There was reason for hope: a major milestone toward First Nations peoples' recognition came in 1967, with a solidly passed referendum recognising Indigenous Australians as citizens.[38] In 1971, for the first time, First Nations Australians were included in the census. It had taken nearly 200 years. The significance of their inclusion went far beyond symbolism: data collection is power, and for the first time, governments and the Australian people would be held accountable for the chasm – in child mortality, education, health, wealth and life expectancy – between the Indigenous and non-Indigenous communities.

Sadly, half a century later, First Nations Australians are still being pushed to the fringes by paternalistic policies and practices introduced long after the passing of the Racial Discrimination Act. Police negatively profile First Nations Australians, leading to serious harassment and discrimination. Indigenous Australians, both children and adults, are over-represented in the criminal justice system and experience injury and deaths at the hands of law enforcement while in custody.[39] Keenan Mundine, director of Inside Out Aboriginal Justice Consultancy, recounts his experience of growing up in Redfern, in inner Sydney, where he says being Aboriginal was on par with committing a crime. 'I remember … being pulled over in family cars and being harassed on the way to school and being searched – and this is before I was committing crime.'[40]

Much doggedness and hard work on the part of First Nations Australians has resulted in change for the good, but white Australia's progress has been slow. Noonuccal's coming dawn of change is still a dream, not yet a reality. This remains a work in progress, unfinished business for the Australian nation.

Immigration to Australia is now much more ethnically diverse than ever before. We now have a demand-driven, skills-based scheme, designed to meet the needs of the national economy, and Indian and Chinese nationals take out the top two spots on the immigration numbers leaderboard. People moving to Australia even in the short term call Australia home and contribute to the country's economic wellbeing, regardless of whether they go on to become citizens.

Yet despite the official end to Australia's racially discriminatory practice of only allowing migration of white Europeans, a restrictive policy of sorts continues to reflect Australia's preference that prospective migrants be educated, English-speaking and wealthy. And the political environment is one that feeds xenophobic populism, at considerable cost to the nation, to win elections.

*

Australia has a long and continuous history of migration, starting with the voyages of First Nations peoples to Sahul many thousands of years ago. Early migratory patterns and the continuing influence of migration are still evident in the peopling and peoples of Australia. Contemporary immigration policies and social conditions relating to First Nations Australians reflect the history of policies and practices past. In examining the peopling of Australia we can look to demography to understand and learn from the past. The past helps us understand the now. Demography thus enables lessons learned and insights captured. Whether mistakes of the past are made over again can only be understood by considering our present demography, who we are now. But first, an earnest lesson in demography.

CHAPTER 2

From the cradle to the grave

What gives life meaning? Ask this question of someone older than yourself, maybe 20 years older. After a prolonged silence, and dumbfounded looks of despair as they search for an answer that makes even half a bit of sense, they might tell you that life is about family. This common response sounds simple, but it's not. By 'family', most people mean achieving and sustaining the traditional familial set-up in our society, and all that it entails: relationship formation, home ownership, babies, raising children. We have a strong desire to leave something of ourselves behind in the world when we've gone, to feel that we've contributed to the future, and having a family is seen as a way of doing just that. Surely there's more to life than having kids, though? Perhaps it's more about what we leave behind, the mark we make on the world: good or bad, big or small.

Gender is a central element of this traditional notion of life and family, a silent yet pervasive social construct. We're born into a world of expectations about the roles of women and men and then conditioned to conform to these roles. Whether we like it or not. No other social norm is quite as entrenched, nor as socially contagious – through observation and interaction – as gender. The way we come to know and perform gender norms is almost unconscious.

Family get-togethers are a good example of this sort of thing, a kind of microcosm of life, showing how social expectations and gendered norms are perpetuated and enforced. Women will particularly relate to being pressured by prying relatives – sometimes even people they barely know – wanting to know personal details about fertility and family planning. Or perhaps you're known as the 'breeder' in your family – a term reserved for women with more than a couple of children. Among the worst questions anyone could possibly be asked is the irritating (and violence-inducing) 'So, are you going to have another baby?' This question is asked of a woman no less than five minutes after she's given birth.

As a demographer, though, I can't really criticise these nosy friends and relatives for wanting to know if you're having another baby and asking how many children you plan to have. Demographers want to know the answers to these questions too. In fact, we need to know the answers to do our jobs. I've promised to tell you the story of us, from cradle to grave, with all the important bits in between, and to do that I have to ask these questions, starting at the very beginning – with the egg.

The ovarian lottery

We all like to think that where we are today and what we've achieved is a result of our own hard work: where we live, the car we drive, the clothes we wear, the possessions we own, our education, the kind of job we do, everything, right down to our health. But what we have and how we see ourselves isn't so much about our hard work but rather what has been bestowed on us. To explain our lives in the present day, we need to trace back through the past, through generation after generation of our ancestors.

It's a simple fact that some of us are luckier than others. The unlucky ones are certainly aware of this disparity. The lucky ones – those who have won what Warren Buffet refers to as the 'ovarian lottery' – may not fully appreciate their own good fortune.[1] Advantage is a matter of chance – the socioeconomic path of our lives is determined by that of our parents. Now, I'm not suggesting you aren't a hard worker. But reality says that your achievements aren't chiefly the result of hard work – they're much more the result of where you started in life than what you've done since: upward social mobility between generations is a lot harder than you'd think.[2] (In fact, it's almost impossible.) On average, we are the apple fallen from the tree.

Let's consider, for a moment, a really basic representation of the course of a human life. A couple of hand-drawn lines. Along the horizontal axis is age, or the total span of our lives – from the cradle to the grave. The vertical axis is the ladder of opportunity, and the nought and cross represent different positions or rungs on that ladder. The rung of opportunity we're born on is our starting position and significantly influences how far we'll climb (or fall) over the course of our lives.

FIGURE 2.1 The course of a human life

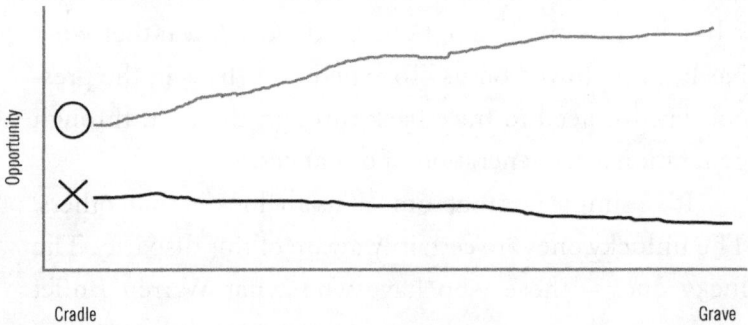

Your biological parents might have hooked up over a cheeky drink, been working hard for a long time to conceive you, or grown you in a lab. However you were conceived, your physical health is determined largely by your genes. The other determining factor is environment, which may activate or 'switch on' certain genes, such as those for obesity or type 2 diabetes. The split between genes and environment in determining what demographers call 'health outcomes' is anywhere from 50/50 to 70/30, with genes making the largest contribution.[3] Sometimes your genes may never be activated in such a way as to produce a particular outcome. But they're there, and often they're just awaiting the right trigger to switch them on.

The circumstances of your birth and the socioeconomic characteristics of your parents are strong predictors of the two main building blocks of success in life: health and education.[4] Health and education in early life are determined by the rung upon which you were born on the ladder of life. That's the reality of society as it stands, anyway.

Take the nought and cross on the chart again. The cross denotes a lower level of socioeconomic opportunity than the nought. A clear disparity is evident at the start of life, and as the differences in education and health compound over time, the disparities seen at birth widen. This is not because the nought worked hard and the cross didn't. It's about access to opportunity. Opportunities depend on where one lives, the amount of money one has, and the network of relationships one can draw on. These disparities are already apparent before a child even presents at school between the ages of four and six – not due to failures on a caregiver's part, but to societal structures that favour those on the higher rungs of the ladder.

It's a brutal thing to acknowledge that we are not all born with the same opportunities, and that the socioeconomic circumstances we're born into can diverge further over the course of our lives, driving a wedge between the different rungs of our society. This is not new knowledge. And regardless of what we like to think, Australia is a class-based society; education and health are just two ways in which it is very evident.[5] If you're still not convinced that it's the ovarian lottery that gets you places, rather than your own hard work ... well, you may have won the ovarian jackpot. I didn't win big myself, but I've made good with my meagre takings.

There are ways to improve our chances in the inevitable lottery of life, and understanding human development is one of them. This understanding can help us to shape the policy and sociocultural structures that contribute to – but can also help to ameliorate – the disparities present at birth.

How we grow and develop

In the 1970s, the Russian-American psychologist Urie Bronfenbrenner developed a model describing the complex interaction between wider social, economic and political structures, individual biological characteristics and family circumstances, and individual outcomes.[6] His 'Ecological Model for Human Development' describes a set of dynamic, hierarchical, concentric influences that shape our lives.[7] According to this model, our lives are the outcome of constrained options.[8] While the original model was used to explain the interactions of the multilevel systems that influence human development, the Bronfenbrenner model has since been used by scholars working in other disciplines to explain a wide range of social phenomena.

Bronfenbrenner's hypothesis is that people do not exist in a social vacuum, free of external influences; instead, we live within a set of nested structures, 'each inside the next, like a set of Russian dolls'.[9] In other words, the individual's human development is a product of their family environment, which is itself a product of the social, eco-nomic and political 'ecology' in which they operate.

The Ecological Model of Human Development com-prises four nested systems – the microsystem, mesosystem, exosystem and macrosystem – each embedded within and bound by another. The model is commonly depicted as a series of concentric circles or a rainbow, as in Figure 2.2.

FIGURE 2.2 Adaptation of Bronfenbrenner's model of human development

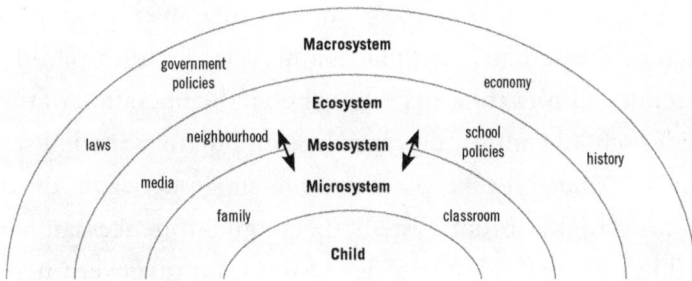

The *microsystem* is the most immediate in which a child participates. Development is shaped by day-to-day personal interactions with others in the family home, such as parents and siblings, and in the classroom, such as teachers and peers.[10] Behaviours and norms are learned from the people the child interacts with on a daily basis, in the course of everyday activities that are determined by the socioeconomic circumstances of the child's family. Even though the microsystem is the environment within which the child develops, it is influenced and affected by the systems operating above it in the hierarchy. These higher-order systems also contribute to or determine individual outcomes, though indirectly.

The *mesosystem* is a set of microsystems comprising the interactions and interrelations between the settings where the developing individual is an active participant. Interactions between the child's parents and teachers, and between their siblings and peers, are examples of such interconnections between systems.

The *exosystem* describes the broader external environment, in which the developing individual is not directly active and which they have no influence over. Examples include the parents' workplaces and social circle, the child's extended family, their neighbourhood, the operation of the wider school community, and exposure to mass media.

The *macrosystem*, as the name suggests, is the overarching higher-order system that both influences and is influenced by the lower-order systems. Laws, government policies, economic systems, history, culture and social conditions all combine to form the macrosystem. Importantly, there is no single macrosystem under which all people function – the individual's macrosystem is unique, shaped by the social groups and subcultures of which they are a member.

Put simply, development occurs at the intersection between family and broader society.[11] We are the product of the environments we grow within.

How we know what we think we know

Data provides a powerful barometer of life. In Australia, the national Census of Population and Housing is one of our most crucial sources of data. Held every five years, the census is the benchmark against which other data collections are measured, to determine how representative they are of the population as a whole. There are, however, other sources that provide information about population change. For example, vital statistics relating to births, deaths, marriages and divorces come from state registries. When a baby is born, or a person dies, when marriages are conducted and divorces occur, state and territory registry offices collect data about these events.

Take the New South Wales Registry of Births, Deaths and Marriages, for example. The registry must be notified of the birth of every baby born in New South Wales, typically by their parents, within 60 days. Information about the newborn (name, date of birth, weight, siblings, and place of birth) and their parents (names, addresses, ages, occupations, relationship, countries of birth, and Indigenous status) is collected as part of the registration process. Many of these details appear on the child's birth certificate – a vital document, without which a person cannot register with Medicare or for welfare payments, enrol in school or open a bank account.

The various state and territory registries are also notified of deaths, typically by funeral directors, and a record is kept of death certificates issued by medical practitioners.

Deaths must be registered within a week of burial or cremation and the details required include name, age, address, Indigenous status, occupation, marital status, children and parents.

If a couple wants to get married, they must first lodge an intention of marriage, to determine their eligibility – that is, to establish that they're adults, and not already married. Nope, drive-through weddings are not allowed in Australia. Names, birth details, occupations, addresses, previous marital status and each partner's parents' names are provided to the registry office by the wedding celebrant, along with details of the marriage ceremony. If a marriage ends in divorce, that too must be registered, but the court is involved in this process.

Data about migration is also collected, but at a national level, using records supplied by Australian immigration ports, mostly airports. The primary aim of this collection is to administer international border movements in and out of Australia.

When data on births, deaths and migration (and to a lesser extent marriages and divorces) is gathered together, this information helps demographers to understand both current population levels and how they are changing. Unfortunately, though, the different state and territory registry offices collect different data, meaning that the data isn't always directly comparable. It falls short in some other important ways, too, failing to fully reflect the lives of all Australians.

This failure is clearest in the case of First Nations Australians, who were deliberately excluded from official data collections in the past. It wasn't until 1966 that Indigenous births were included in national data, and 1971 that Indigenous people were counted in the census. Even after provisions were put in place to address under-registration of vital events among First Nations communities, births of Indigenous people went unregistered in large numbers until the 1990s. In fact, Indigenous births still go unregistered today, which is troubling when, as noted above, possession of a birth certificate is what determines access to social services and entrance into school. Data relating to Indigenous deaths is highly problematic too, because Indigenous status is reported by doctors certifying the death or funeral directors making the report, who don't necessarily think to ask the family about the deceased's Indigenous status – and even when they do, the response may not reflect the deceased's self-identification.

But why do we need all this data? And what use is it? The answer is that this data contains useful information about what the future might hold – but only if we know how to interpret it. Without interpretation, data remains just data, and never becomes information.

For example, ten births could occur in town A and 110 births in town B over the same period. On the face of it, town B appears to have a much higher fertility than town A. We can't draw this conclusion, however, unless we know the size of the population in each town and the age and sex composition of those populations. Town A might have a much smaller and younger population, making its overall fertility rate higher than that of Town B.

Data can't be taken at face value – it must be examined in context to be useful. To interpret data, demographers rely on theoretical models that help us make sense of it, so that's what we'll look at next.

Transitions and change

Demographers like to talk about three overarching 'transitions': the demographic, epidemiologic and nutrition transitions. These are theories or models of change developed through observation of past events, and together they are useful tools in interpreting and managing current and future change.

The theory of demographic transition is integral to the interpretation of population dynamics and to the study of demography more generally. This model is used to explain the shift from historically high mortality and fertility rates to today's relatively low rates, a result of economic and technological advancement.[12] Traditionally, demographic transition is thought to have four stages: pre-transition; followed by two transitional stages, the first marked by a decline in mortality and the second by a decline in fertility; and then a final, post-transition state.[13] This four-step transition was first described by American demographer Warren Thompson in 1929, based on his study of changes observed in western European societies between 1800 and the 1930s. The model was further developed by other theorists, and was given its current name in 1945.

During pre-transition – the high mortality and high

fertility stage – life expectancy is low. Population growth is very slow, because births and deaths are balanced. Having lots of babies is the norm, which is partly the result of religious and social conventions, but also due to a lack of family planning, the need for a large agricultural work-force, and the fact that children are seen as economic assets to the family. High mortality is due to malnutrition and high levels of infectious disease, exacerbated by unsafe drinking water, poor sanitation and garbage disposal, and competition for food with pests. Poor access to health care and education are contributing factors, as are famine and war. Somalia is an example of a pre-transition population, with high fertility, mortality and population growth.

The second phase, in which mortality declines while fertility remains high, is accompanied by changes in agri-cultural production, industry and society generally, includ-ing urbanisation, increasing literacy, growing affluence and the waning influence of religion on daily life.[14] When mortality declines yet fertility remains high, the population grows: there are more human lives incoming than out-going. Mortality among children and women, especially, shows the greatest improvements. The result is a larger population, and a younger one, creating opportunities to invest in the education and training of the future workforce, paving the way for an economic boom – the demographic dividend that I discussed in the preface. Life expectancy also increases, moving from a low of around 20 to 40 years to somewhere between 50 and 65 years.[15] Factors leading to a decline in mortality include improved sanitation and safe drinking water, the introduction of waste management services, improved health care (especially access to surgery and better infection control), immunisation, child and maternal health, greater food security (better production, transport and storage), safer working conditions and improvements in living conditions generally.

In the third phase, fertility also declines. The average number of children being born per family drops, and population growth slows. But the so-called fertility transition isn't just fewer births – it's a revolution. As couples are granted control of their fertility, there are also fewer unintended pregnancies and more space between births. This control leads to delayed (older) parenthood, and greater numbers of people choosing not to have children at all. This is all thanks to family planning. A lower infant mortality rate also means that families require fewer children to achieve their intended family size. At the same time, automation and mechanisation of labour and production make household duties less arduous. As women's lives change, no longer centred entirely around child rearing but potentially encompassing education and paid work, higher standards of living blossom. An example of a population in transition is Bangladesh, where fertility and mortality are declining and population growth is moderate.

The final phase is post-transition. Australia, like much of the world, now finds itself in this post-transitional stage, marked by low fertility, low mortality and low population growth. In some countries, such as Italy and South Korea, the population is even facing decline. The problem is that we're not having enough children to replace ourselves. ('Replacement fertility' is calculated by establishing how many children, on average, couples need to have to replace themselves, and then adjusting for mortality.[16]) Over half the world now experiences a below-replacement fertility rate of 2.1 live births per woman of childbearing age (that is, between 15 and 49 years).[17] We're living longer, too, which means that older people, and particularly those aged over 75 years, represent an ever-increasing proportion of the total population. As a result, we have to rely on immigration to offset the demographic consequences of population ageing. In Germany, for example, the immediate threat of population decline has been offset by immigration: the country has been a world leader in its generous intake of asylum seekers from Syria and Turkey, and is reaping the benefits, in the form of a boost to its working-age population. Australia similarly relies on immigration to counter the effects of a falling birth rate and an ageing population.

The demographic transition model has its limitations, though. Firstly, it's a descriptive model, presenting a simplified representation of reality. It merely describes the changes a society goes through in each of the four stages without seeking to explain the timing of these changes, or their causes. It doesn't, for example, explain what initially causes the decline in mortality when transition first begins. It's also an ethnocentric model, centred on western European societies, and frames change as a kind of evolution; there's an implicit assumption that post-transition societies are more 'advanced' or 'evolved' than pre-transition societies. The model is therefore limited: it can't necessarily be applied to all populations around the world, as societies undergo changes at different times, in different ways and in a different order.

The model isn't sophisticated enough, for example, to describe what's going on with fertility here in Australia. Despite overall fertility declining below replacement level in Australia, the fertility of First Nations Australians is booming. High fertility is a stand-out feature of young indigenous populations in countries with a similar history of invasion and colonisation, such as New Zealand, Canada and the United States.[18] Neither are mortality and life expectancy among First Nations Australians consistent with those of a post-transition population. To understand why, we need to turn to the other theories of transition.

The epidemiologic transition theory was developed in the early 1970s, partly to address the limitations of the demographic transition theory. The epidemiologic model both describes and explains the decline in communicable diseases and famine that occurs in the first transitional phase, and the accompanying rise in non-communicable and degenerative diseases. Crucial to this new theory was the idea that health is an important explanatory factor, even a predictor, facilitating the decline in mortality.[19]

The epidemiologic model has five key principles:

- Mortality is fundamental to understanding population change.

- Degenerative diseases slowly displace infectious pandemics.
- Children and women are those most positively affected by improved health and falling rates of disease.
- Demographic and socioeconomic development are necessary factors that cause (and also result from) these changes.
- Epidemiologic change occurs differently in different populations, according to their stage of demographic transition and level of development.

The process by which infectious diseases give way to degenerative and lifestyle diseases has three stages. In the first stage, infectious and vector-borne diseases (such as malaria, transmitted by mosquitos) are still prevalent. In the second stage, infectious epidemic disease outbreaks gradually recede, giving way to the third stage, in which chronic degenerative diseases and so-called diseases of lifestyle represent the biggest threat. American public health experts Stuart Jay Olshansky and Brian Ault propose a fourth stage, in which the onset of degenerative diseases is delayed, and we live longer and healthier lives.[20] More recently, Michael Gaziano, an American public health specialist, has proposed a fifth stage: an age of obesity and inactivity, during which life expectancy declines due to the unhealthy way we live our lives, a result of changes in food production and consumption, and in our use of technology. Most developed countries are now entering this so-called fifth stage.[21]

But while the demographic and epidemiologic transition models go some way towards describing historical patterns of change in a population's health and wellbeing, the nutrition transition theory goes beyond this. This model actually explains transition as the result of changing production and consumption of food, leading, eventually, to an increase in the incidence of overweight and obesity. Interestingly, overweight and obesity are just as much an issue of malnutrition as underweight. Underweight often results at least in part from undernutrition and overweight is in many cases a result of overnutrition.[22]

The nutrition transition model identifies five stages of food production and consumption. Like the demographic and epidemiologic transitions, the nutrition transition occurs differently, and at different times, in different countries. The differential is largely determined by a country's income. The five stages are: collecting food, famine, receding famine, degenerative disease, and behavioural change. These stages are used to explain the shift from a subsistence lifestyle, characterised by severe food insecurity and malnutrition, to increased food security and better nutrition, followed by a gradual move towards the production of more convenient and more highly refined foods, and ending with a move to healthier foods and increased physical activity.

So, let's bring on the data!

It's plain to see the phenomenal transformation Australia has experienced by plotting that change on a graph. Figure 2.3 shows what the nation has lived through in the period from Federation to the recent past – in population terms, anyway. Everything from world wars, economic booms and busts, infectious pandemics, the introduction of reliable birth control and no-fault divorce, to conflicts in far-off lands can be seen in the peaks and troughs in this graph. You might be looking at the graph and thinking *How? Where?* Well, let's take a closer look.

FIGURE 2.3 Components of population change, Australia, 1901–2018[23]

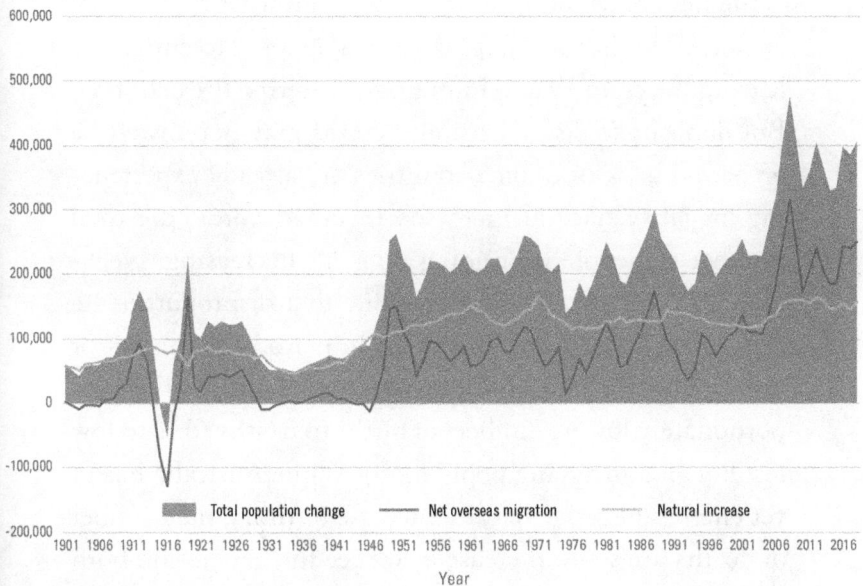

NOTE Data do not include accurate Indigenous population figures until 1971, and Indigenous births have only been recorded since 1966.

Remember the three major components of population change demographers talk about: births, deaths and migration? Together, these three can be used to measure overall population change – the bottom line or quantum of how a population changes year on year. Looking solely at births or solely at deaths is interesting, but it tells us little about how these two population dynamics contribute to change. If we consider instead the difference between the number of people born and the number of people dying, we come up with what's known as 'natural increase'. Natural increase is the net contribution to the overall numbers that can be attributed to the local population (as opposed to emigrants leaving the country and immigrants entering the country). But don't be fooled – natural increase may not always be an actual increase. Some countries are already experiencing 'negative natural increase'. In other words, the total number of people isn't going up – it's decreasing. Negative natural increase can occur due to a disproportionate number of deaths over births (as in periods of conflict or during major infectious outbreaks), or as a result of disproportionately lower numbers of births to deaths (due to low fertility and an ageing population). While Australia hasn't yet entered negative natural increase territory, the number of deaths are set to increase as we see the generation born during the baby boom after World War II enter the peak ages of mortality. But more on that later.

On the other side of the population equation is migration. Migration can occur internally from town to town or state to state, as well as internationally. Again, knowing the net contribution is important in calculating changes to a population. Net internal migration matters when we look at subnational population estimates – such as the population of Sydney or New South Wales, for example – because local government planning and provision relies on knowing population needs. When we're considering national figures, our main interest lies in net international migration: the difference between the number of people coming in and the number leaving.

Definitions are important here. In Australia, we talk about 'temporary migration' and 'permanent migration'. Both contribute to population counts, because we need to know the number of people in need of services at any one time. Temporary migration figures measure the number of non-citizens present in Australia who have been granted a temporary visa and intend to stay here for twelve months or more. Permanent migration figures measure the number of people who have been granted permanent residency in Australia. Once a person has been granted permanent residency, they're on route to gaining Australian citizenship. Not all permanent residents will become citizens, but most do. Not every visitor or holiday-maker is included in the population data: people who usually live in another country and intend to stay here less than a year are classed as 'overseas visitors', not temporary migrants.[24]

Together, natural increase and net overseas migration add up to a figure known as the 'estimated resident population', affectionately referred to as ERP. Estimated resident population is precisely that – an estimate. In the years between censuses, the ERP is calculated using demographic formulas, taking census data as a starting point or benchmark.

But let's get back to our graph again. Figure 2.3 shows that since Federation, natural increase has usually been the greatest contributor to overall population growth. Notable exceptions include the periods following the world wars, and the years since 2005. In the 13 years from 2005 to 2018, net overseas migration was the largest contributor to overall population change. This departure from historical trends reflects declining fertility and an ageing population. New waves of net overseas migration help keep the population younger, by bolstering the age cohorts among the peak working-age population.

The most interesting thing about figure 2.3, though, is what it *doesn't* show us. Take net overseas migration. The line on the chart shows us the rate of change. Over a quarter of Australia's population is now born overseas: 26 per cent as at 2016.[25] In 1966, following the peak post-war immigration intake, this figure was just 18 per cent. We can see the number of migrants going up and down on the chart – but what we can't see is where those migrants come from. This is where census data comes in. The data allows us to go deeper, investigating such questions as the typical migrant's country of origin at different points in our history. Throughout most of the period since Federation, migrants from England and New Zealand were the biggest group, but a look at the people who've migrated more recently shows us that China and India are becoming more prominent as countries from which Australia draws migrants. This is a significant departure from historical precedent, beginning only in the 1980s.[26] Australia's cultural diversity today is spectacular. Australians hail from over 190 countries worldwide. We're even more diverse when you factor in all the hundreds of First Nations cultures, with their own languages and stories, that have been here from the start.

Just as the line showing net overseas migration doesn't convey the full story behind the statistics, the natural increase trend also hides a phenomenally powerful story. The births component of natural increase is expressed as a number – but a mere number cannot and does not say anything about who these babies are being born to. Fertility rates, on the other hand, take this information into account, counting births per age group, and not just all births to all women of reproductive age. As we'll soon see, there's a hidden story here – the story of the spectacular empowerment of women over the past century.

Fertility rates are calculated by looking at a specific section of the population: namely, women aged between 15 and 49 years. Demographers describe women in this age group as being 'at risk' of a birth. In times past, fertility rates were calculated for married women separately from unmarried women, and surveys tracking 'fertility intentions' (the number of children women wanted) included only married women. These data were referred to as nuptial fertility (or births), or conversely, ex-nuptial fertility (or births). Because, apparently, only married women had sex and were at risk of having babies. Obviously, we know this not to be the case. It's hard not to laugh at those who ever entertained such notions. Even more troubling for me, as a never-married woman demographer with children, is that the United Nations *still* refers to babies born outside of marriage as 'illegitimate' in their annual Yearbook. But I digress.

The total fertility rate calculation isn't about lifetime fertility of, say, a cohort of women born in a particular year. Instead, it's a retrospective measure of fertility during a specific period, using data from that period. For example, if 2017 is the year under consideration, an age-specific fertility rate is established for that year for women aged between 15 and 49 years. The *total* fertility rate indicates the average number of children a woman in a given population will have over her lifetime, if the age-specific fertility rates current in 2017 remain current throughout her life. This indicator hides child-free and childless women, and also female fecundity. In the popular vernacular, 'fertility' and 'fecundity' mean more or less the same thing, but not in world of demography. For demographers, fertility is a measure of how many children an individual has, and fecundity is the biophysical capability to have children. You can see from the language used here that demography kind of has a problem with gender, and the realities of life.

Figure 2.4 illustrates changes in Australia's total fertility rate between 1935 and 2017. If you know how to read it, you'll see a picture of historical, cultural and social change. It should be noted, though, that the chart doesn't tell us the full story: First Nations births weren't typically included in the calculation of the national fertility rate until after 1966. The key trends in total fertility rates reflect responses to local and global influences: a relative low during World War II (which came off a high following World War I); a major uptick in the years after World War II, leading into a boom, culminating in the highest period of fertility recorded during the window of analysis; a demographic rebound, and a steady decline following major policy reforms; and finally a plateau of below-replacement-level fertility.

Even in the absence of reliable reproductive technology, individuals and couples have always sought to control the number of children they have. Take the World War II period, for example. Men were called away to fight at the

FIGURE 2.4 Total fertility rate, Australia, 1935–2017[27]

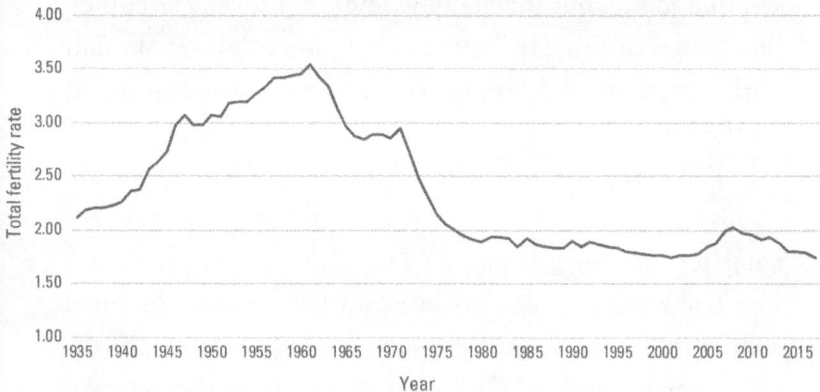

NOTE Indigenous births have only been recorded since 1966.

peak of their reproductive years, which was also the peak of their working years, many leaving the country to never return. Women were called on to fill the vacancies left by men – in the workplace and in society generally – and childbearing was put off because men were absent. The mobilisation of women would eventually lead to changes in social norms governing women's participation in paid employment – but not before they went backwards for about 20 years. Following World War II, men returned home and most married women were forced to resume their traditional place in the private sphere.

Populate! was the mantra in the period following World War II. Figure 2.3 shows how dutiful Australians were to the cause. Fertility rates soared. The male-breadwinner model ruled, enshrined in policy, theoretically ensuring economic prosperity for all. Technology in the home was coming along, but for many women housework occupied vast hours of the day. Between running a household and caring for kids and family, women's time was consumed by the home.

Following the so-called economic golden age of the 1950s and peak fertility in 1961 of 3.6 births per woman, total fertility rates began to fall. The decline was swift and irreversible. Between 1961 and 1971 fertility dropped markedly. There was a slight rebound in 1971, to 3.0 births per woman, but by 1976 they had plummeted below the replacement level of 2.1, for all the reasons we've already discussed, including access to the pill, no-fault divorce and increased female participation in work and education. And below replacement level is where total fertility rates have stayed since, only coming close to 2.1 births per woman again briefly in 2008.

I can imagine what you're thinking. Firstly, what about all the pronatalist policies and programs Australia has had since the 2000s? Well, they had little to do with boosting fertility in any substantive way. It was a matter of demography: the age structure of the female population was such that a bit of a rebound was expected.[28] Sorry, Peter Costello – you had nothing to do with it! In 2004, during his time as federal treasurer, Costello urged Australians: 'You should have one for the father, one for the mother and one for the country'[29] – but somehow that didn't motivate Australians to get busy procreating. Who would have thought Costello's face plastered all over the media alongside oodles of babies wouldn't turn people on?

Secondly, I suspect you're thinking: *Well, so what?*

Individuals and couples having greater control over their own fertility is a good thing – especially as we know that control over fertility means women are no longer tied to the home, freeing them to participate in paid work. It's an equality thing.

Breaking down the total fertility rate – the births per woman over a lifetime – to focus on age-specific rates, it's very clear delayed childbearing is occurring. That is, women are participating in further education and building careers, but they're still having children, too, albeit fewer of them. Figure 2.5 traces the historical trend, expressed as the number of births per 1000 women, from 1935 to 2017.

What stands out is the change in the birth rate for women aged between 30 and 34. Women in this group had the third highest rate of births of all the reproductive age ranges from 1935 right up until the mid-to-late 1980s. Prior to this crossover point, women aged between 20 and 29 years had the highest rate of births. Then, in the early 2000s, women aged between 30 and 34 overtook them. This became the norm, and it has remained so ever since.

The importance of delayed childbearing is multi-faceted, but its most significant outcome is the reduced

FIGURE 2.5 Age-specific fertility rate, Australia, 1935–2017[30]

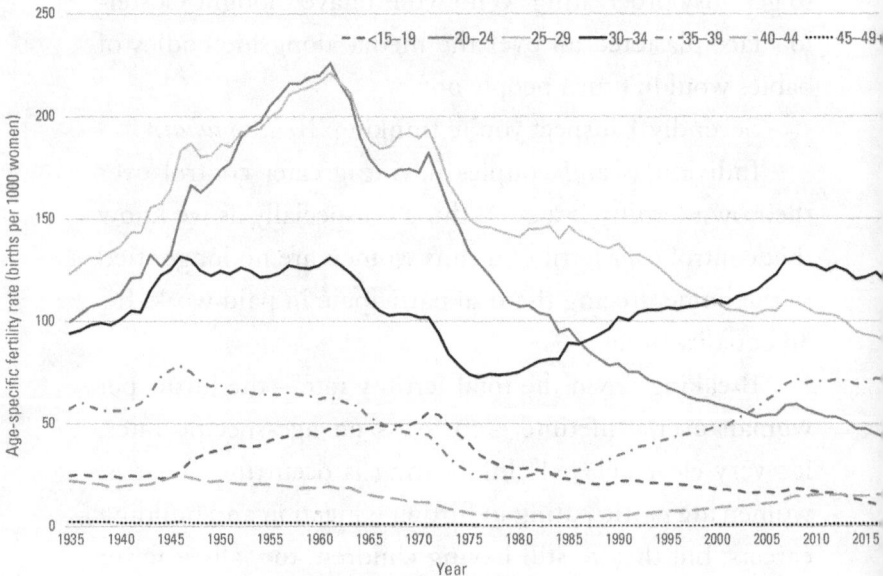

NOTE Indigenous births have only been recorded since 1966.

window it gives women (and their partners) first to have a child and then to go on and have more, if they choose. Data from a nationally representative longitudinal survey confirms this: women and their partners are having fewer children than they intend, because, well, life gets in the way.[31] An entire industry has sprung up in response, trying to frighten women, particularly younger women, into freezing and storing their eggs as an insurance policy against declining or totally depleted fecundity when it comes time to start a family. It's a predatory industry, playing on women's deepest fears, and it rakes in the cash, despite limited evidence of its success.

So far I've looked at the overall statistics about fertility and population change for the nation as a whole, but a vital, and often undiscussed, contributor to Australia's total fertility is that of Indigenous women. Figure 2.6 offers an age-specific breakdown of Indigenous women's fertility in 2017, comparing it with Australia's total fertility in the same year and also at the postwar peak in 1961.

While the total fertility rate of all Australian women is a story right out of the demographic transition model manual, the fertility of First Nations women is an entirely different story. Kim Johnstone, a New Zealand-born demographer, suggests that the pattern of fertility among First Nations women is more a story of stalled fertility transition.[32] Rather than a stalled transition, I'd suggest that the primacy of family in First Nations communities is the most likely explanatory factor for what Figure 2.6 shows. This primacy is expressed as a preference for larger families, a family-centric culture driving a desire for children, and familial support networks which ease the burden of caregiving. Fertility among First Nations women takes on a pattern of age-specific fertility resembling that of the stage before post-transition for all Australian women. While the quantum is not the same, the peak childbearing years are similar, falling in women's twenties, rather than their thirties. This means the window of potential childbearing is greater for First Nations women than it is for other Australian women, which is reflected in the higher total fertility rate of 2.3 births per Indigenous woman, compared to 1.74 births for all women.[33]

FIGURE 2.6 Age-specific fertility rate by Indigenous status and total women, Australia, 1961 and 2017[34]

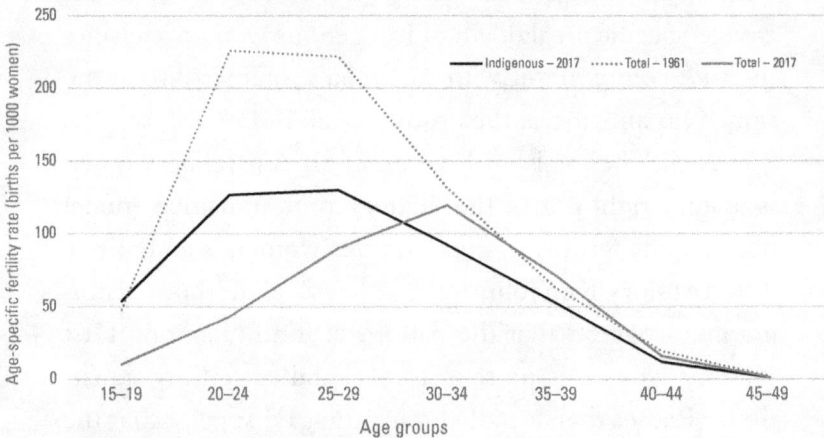

NOTE Indigenous births have only been recorded since 1966.

Higher fertility among First Nations women presents opportunities, in the form of a demographic dividend: as Australia's overall population ages, Indigenous Australians will be in an advantageous position, demographically speaking, in the economy. This demographic dividend comes from the bulk of people being at peak working age. But barriers need to be smashed to prevent the discriminatory practices we see today that limit access to education and culturally appropriate health care, among other things.

Another significant area of disparity between First Nations and non-Indigenous Australians is life expectancy at birth. Just like the total fertility rate, life expectancy at birth uses retrospective data for a period of time. Life expectancy at birth provides an indication of the average life years babies born in a particular year might live if age-specific death rates of that year hold over their lifetime.

Life expectancy at birth has increased markedly in Australia since data on this subject was first collected around 1881. Unfortunately, the data are limited when it comes to First Nations Australians. In 1971, average life expectancy at birth was 68 years for Australian men and 75 for Australian women.[35] Fast-forward to 2017, and life expectancy for males had increased by just over 12 years for men, to 81, and by 10 years for women, to 85.[36] While male life expectancy showed the greatest increase in this period, the longer view, looking back to the late 1800s and using the first available data, shows that women have experienced a greater overall increase than men (34 years for women, versus 33 years for men), up from a life expectancy of

50.9 for women and 47.2 years for men. The overall increase in life expectancy at birth has been largely due to declining infant mortality, and particularly deaths occurring soon after birth.

While these advances in life expectancy should be celebrated, it should also be noted that First Nations Australians, men and women, have a shorter life expectancy than their non-Indigenous counterparts. In both cases, it's a gap of nine years: Indigenous men have an average life expectancy of 72 years, and for Indigenous women it's 76 years.[37] Comparing Australians' overall life expectancy at birth and that of First Nations peoples is like comparing Australia with Bangladesh.

But while there is an enormous gap in life expectancy at birth between First Nations and non-Indigenous Australians, there isn't such a great difference between all Australian men and all Australian women. A closer look at the underlying differences in age-specific death rates between men and women reveals what might be at play here.

Figure 2.7 traces age-specific death rates in five-year age groups from birth to 100 years and over, clearly showing the disparity between men and women (using a logarithmic scale to highlight the difference).

The time immediately around an individual's birth is the riskiest for males under 30 years and females under 35 years. Being born is risky. It's even riskier for males than for females, if only by a little. This is considered to be the result of biophysical differences between the sexes, and that is why, in a population free of sex-selective birth

FIGURE 2.7 Age-specific death rates, Australia, 2017[38]

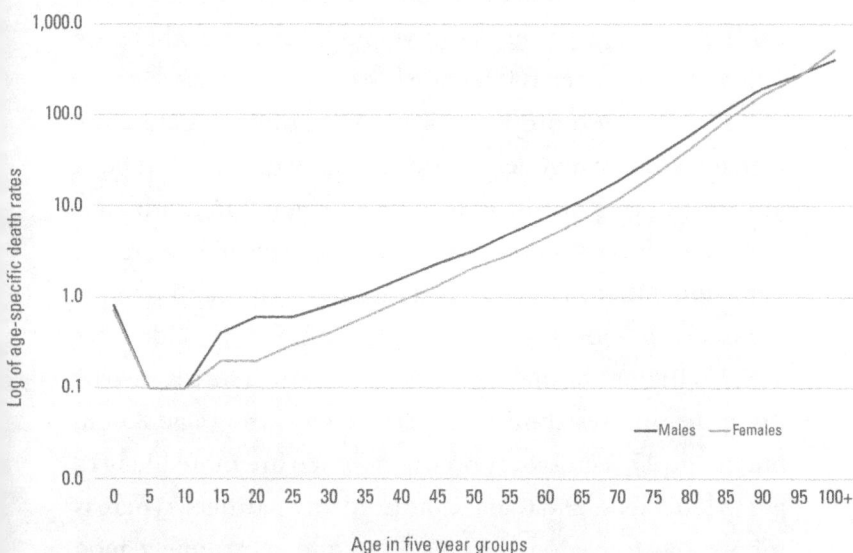

practices, more males are born than females. The sex ratio at birth is normally 105 males to every 100 females – thought to be nature's way of ensuring that there are equal numbers of males and females as each generation reaches childbearing age. In countries where sex-selective practices exist (such as India and China), the imbalance between male and female births is evident, and so too is the difficulty of relationship formation as men outnumber women later in life.[39] In 2017, for example, 115 males were born per 100 females in China; the figure was 111 males per 100 females in India.[40] Worldwide, it's estimated that tens of millions of girls are missing from the population due to sex-selective practices including abortion, in-vitro selection and infanticide. Even in Australia, there's some evidence to suggest sex-selective practices occur: there are 106 male births per 100 female births.

Risk of death drops markedly in the period before the teenage years, when deaths are at the lowest they will be at any time during the life span. The divergence in death rates from age 15 is extremely telling. Males typically engage in behaviours that involve greater risk than girls, and parents are likely to allow boys greater freedom, too. Suicide rates are also higher for males in this age group. The sex disparity in death rates continues, yet narrows, from age 25 on, but at age 95, a crossover occurs. Women are more likely to get to later ages, and to have outlived any partners, whereas men who survive to later ages do so due to extremely good health.

You might think the differences in mortality over a lifetime can be explained just as they are at the start: due to biophysical differences. But this is not the case. Yes, biophysical factors are at play to some degree, but social factors are likely more prominent. Greater risk-taking, dangerous employment, higher substance use (including tobacco), heart disease, reluctance to seek medical care, greater body mass, higher rates of suicide and fewer social connections are thought to account for the disparities in mortality from childhood.[41] This is despite the fact that women experience greater levels of social exclusion, mental illness and stress, intimate partner violence and social inequality.

*

Where we are today is a complex story of where we've been and how we came to be, both as individuals and as a population. But what's next? If the past is anything to go by, fertility will continue to decline, or at the very least stabilise below replacement. Mortality could increase, especially between the ages of 50 to 70, resulting in a decline in life expectancy, similar to that which has already been observed in the United States and United Kingdom. As populations age, migration will play an increasing role in the socioeconomic wellbeing of Australia. Exactly what that looks like and how it comes to pass, and the likely social consequences, need to be carefully considered.

The now – our current situation – and the challenges and opportunities it presents, are what we'll consider next, in Part II: 'The problem with us'.

PART II

The problem with us

CHAPTER 3

Modern demography

Contemporary societies the world over like to think they're in a period of post-enlightenment. Getting on with the job of being smart and innovative leaders in the global marketplace. But what are the defining features of a modern demography? And are we really as smart as we like to think we are? Well, it depends where in the world we focus. Australia's contemporary population and its demographic composition are unique in some ways. Yet at the same time, we share striking similarities with some other countries in the world. Low fertility, increased life expectancy and a reliance on overseas migration are features of many countries across the world today. But if Australia had to nominate one demographic twin, it would have to be Canada. Both countries have a strong migration program, each built by reflecting on lessons learned from the other. Canada and Australia have similar, yet different, colonisation stories, and indigenous populations who experience continuing disadvantage and discrimination.

Reflecting upon the demographic circumstances of countries beyond Australia is vital to our future prospects.

Most importantly, by looking beyond us and out to the world, we can better understand the challenges and opportunities we face. If we look at policy and practice tried and tested by other countries, we won't just know what to do – we'll know what *not* to do too. At the same time, policy and practice must be understood in a global context. It's no good setting a path for one country without considering the situations and trajectories of other countries.

The social, economic and demographic challenges we face today (and tomorrow) should ultimately offer us opportunities, but we have to identify the challenges first, before we can identify those opportunities. Fortunately, demography isn't an overly fast moving beast – population isn't a sudden occurrence, like a lightning bolt out of the blue – so we have a good amount of lead time. There are never any certainties in demography, but some bets are safer than others. With this in mind, let's explore the problem – or rather the problems – with us.

Where Australians live

Whether home is the flood plains of north-west Sydney or the salty mangroves of far-north Queensland, nature informs and restricts our existence. The geographic distribution of the Australian population across the country has been shaped by the natural environment. It has also been shaped by settlement patterns of the past, our labour market and vital infrastructure networks. Many politicians and social commentators have bemoaned the geography of

Australia's population, but few (if any) have done much to understand or address the issue.

Australia's physical landscape is vast and complex. In the north, a long wet season feeds lush rainforests, while much of the centre of Australia is desert. Life exists in the centre, but the traditional custodians' knowledge of how best to live in these areas has not been well understood by a mostly white bureaucracy. The southern girth of the continent is more readily habitable, especially in the south-east, where the climate is kinder and gentler.

Rainfall is unevenly dispersed, and guaranteeing water supplies for drinking and agriculture presents a serious challenge. Our use of freshwater river systems is antiquated and inefficient. The building of dams and siphoning of water from major river systems pit the traditional custodians of the land against industry and aquaculture. These are enduring issues, ones Australia has been notoriously bad at addressing. In recent times, this is perhaps due to the reluctance of governments, at all levels, to recognise the crisis posed by climate change – a worldwide phenomenon to which Australia is especially vulnerable.

The complexity of our climate and the harsh contrasts of our landscape are nicely expressed by Dorothea Mackellar in her famous poem professing love for Australia.[1]

From plains, mountains, rainforests and the sea, Mackellar paints a literary picture of the beauty of the landscape. She points to the contradictions of the land and the hardships these bring in deadly droughts and life-giving rains. Mackellar's love letter to the country describes the blue, sun-filled skies of Australia that carry a uniqueness that sets the nation apart from the rest of the world.

The British colonisers didn't appreciate the unique beauty Mackellar described, nor the extreme contrast of the landscape – something we're still grappling with today. Trees were felled and land cleared indiscriminately as they established the colony, essentially trying to create a 'little England' on Sydney's shores. Buildings were constructed and infrastructure developed without regard for the First Nations peoples already inhabiting the area.

The distribution of Australia's population can be understood by studying the history of invasion and colonisation: Sydney was the initial settlement, and further settlements radiated out from it, along the rivers of the Sydney basin, as larger and larger areas of land were taken from the First Nations peoples. It's no surprise then that the Sydney region, with its long history of European settlement, is still the most populous part of the country.

New South Wales is home to the highest proportion of people living in Australia today (see Table 3.1). In total, over 8 million people call New South Wales home, 32 per cent of the total Australian population. Victoria is the second most populous state, at 26 per cent of the total (6.5 million). Rounding off the top three is Queensland, with 20 per cent of people living in the Sunshine State (5.1 million people). Western Australia, South Australia, Tasmania, the Australian Capital Territory and the Northern Territory share (albeit unequally) the remaining 22 per cent of the Australian population between them.

TABLE 3.1 Population summary statistics by state/territory, Australia, 2018[2]

	NSW	Vic	Qld	SA	WA	Tas	NT	ACT	Australia
:imated sident pulation	8,038,109	6,527,379	5,050,706	1,743,014	2,605,807	531,657	245,523	423,334	25,170,175
are of total stralian pulation)	32	26	20	7	10	2	1	2	100
wth rate	1.5	2.2	1.8	0.8	0.9	1.3	-0.5	1.8	1.6

More telling, perhaps, is the recent rate of growth for each of the states and territories. Victoria is growing the fastest of all, at a rate of 2.2 per cent in the year to December 2018. At 1.8 per cent, Queensland and the much smaller Australian Capital Territory come closest to the Victorian figure. New South Wales is not far behind, at 1.5 per cent. Growth across Australia is mostly due to net overseas migration rather than natural increase or even internal migration.

A closer look at the distribution of Australia's population shows that it is heavily concentrated in urban communities. Across Australia, 72 per cent of people live in major cities, and most live within 50 kilometres of the coast.[3] There is variation between the states and territories, though, as shown in Figure 3.1. The Australian Capital Territory is a particular stand-out, with nearly 100 per cent of people there living in a major city (in other words, in Canberra). Tasmania and the Northern Territory are equally peculiar, with no one at all living in major cities. (Hobart and Darwin don't provide the services that define a major city, and are therefore classified as regional areas.) But leaving these quirky exceptions aside, it's clear people in Australia do like a major city. There's no surprise there, really. Opportunities in major cities far exceed those in regional or remote areas. The sheer number of people living in a major city offers benefits in the way of education, employment and business opportunities, as well as greater access to shops, transport and medical care.

FIGURE 3.1 Estimated resident population by remoteness, Australia, 2018[4]

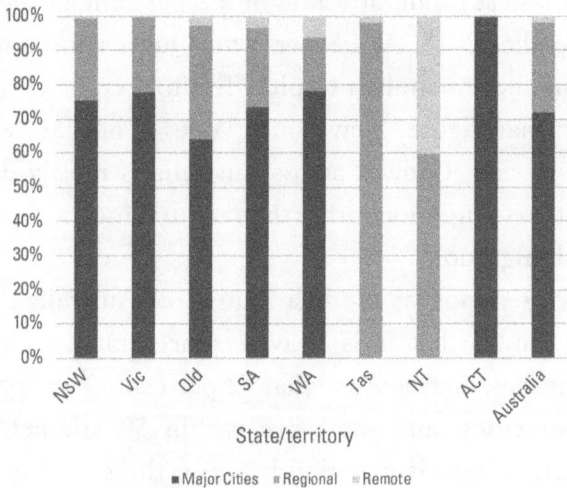

Those of us who live in cities have a definite economic advantage over those living in regional and remote areas, and receive better health care, too. This 'geographic inequality' is largely the result of physical proximity: where we live determines our access to services and opportunities, and their relative cost. The effect of physical proximity on access is best understood in terms of urbanisation, which is a component of the demographic transition model. Remember the first theory of population change we looked at in the last chapter? Yep, that one!

Urbanisation is a slow and ongoing form of migration, and it's been happening the world over for many years now. Like demographic transition, urbanisation is experienced differently by different societies, but one commonality exists: previously predominantly rural populations tend over time to shift towards city living in ever greater numbers. This migration represents a major change, both for society and for the individual migrants. The transition from a rural-agricultural economy to industry and manufacturing is a long one, as economic activity is refocused and then becomes more concentrated as a means of increasing productivity.

As they grow, cities often become crowded and polluted, but their growth also makes possible the development of infrastructure, through economies of scale.[5] Think sewerage, safe drinking water, garbage disposal and the provision of medical care. City living becomes more and more attractive, and as industry and economic activity become concentrated in urban centres, the number of city dwellers continues to grow. Today, urban populations are at the highest levels ever observed. What comes next is anybody's guess. On one hand, highly concentrated city populations might start to disperse. On the other and more likely hand, cities might retain their demographic dominance. Until economic activity is dispersed, populations are unlikely to disperse, and major cities will keep on growing.

Australia was fairly late to the urbanisation transition – big city living was basically unheard of here until the second half of the 20th century. That's not surprising, given the vast size of the continent and the long, bitter process of colonisation. But in the years since, as we've already seen, we've become a nation of city dwellers. Attempts to decentralise our population outside the major cities have so far fallen flat. Instead, economic and educational opportunities have become more and more centralised in urban areas. The greatest and most diverse employment opportunities are also to be found in the major cities of Australia. It's no wonder the majority of us live in a city.

Living longer

Australians are living longer than ever before, and, as I noted in the previous chapter, we're also having fewer children. Both below-replacement fertility and increased longevity are the result of past successes, but together they add up to population ageing, which presents some unique challenges, particularly for the budget bottom line.

Low fertility has been a concern throughout Australian

history, and was even the subject of royal commissions in 1903 and 1944. The first, known as the Mackellar Royal Commission, was held in New South Wales, in response to a government statistician's report that showed fertility was declining. It set the scene for future debates concerning fertility right throughout the 20th century and to the present day. The commissioners learned that couples were struggling with the financial pressures of having children, making larger families prohibitive. Rather than considering how government could better support families, or recognising that smaller families were the new norm, the conservative all-male panel found that selfish hedonism was to blame for declining fertility. People were neglecting their obligations to the community, they said, because they didn't want the worry of children. Women were reluctant to undergo pregnancy and birth; children disrupted people's lives; and a love of 'luxury and social pleasures' had taken hold.[6] Their findings reflected a profound moral panic – but only on the part of the commissioners, it seems, as their concerns were not reflected by the general community. If they were concerned back in 1903, imagine what they'd say looking at our current situation!

Figure 3.2 shows the Australian population's structure by age and sex at 20-year intervals, starting in 1938 and ending with the projected figures for 2038, clearly demonstrating the magnitude of our ageing. In 1938, towards the end of the Great Depression and prior to World War II, the age and sex distribution of the Australian population was more or less a traditional pyramid shape. With almost seven million people and a fertility rate nearing replacement, it's clear that a certain amount of fertility control was occurring. Yes, even in the absence of reliable and accessible contraception. The median age of the Australian population in 1938 was 29 years, and the population pyramid shows a solid chunk of the population in the early years of their labour force participation and reproductive life.

In the 20 years to 1958, Australia underwent massive social, economic and cultural change. And it's evident in the population composition shown in Figure 3.2. Fertility

FIGURE 3.2 Population by age and sex, Australia[7]

Projected population, Australia - 1938

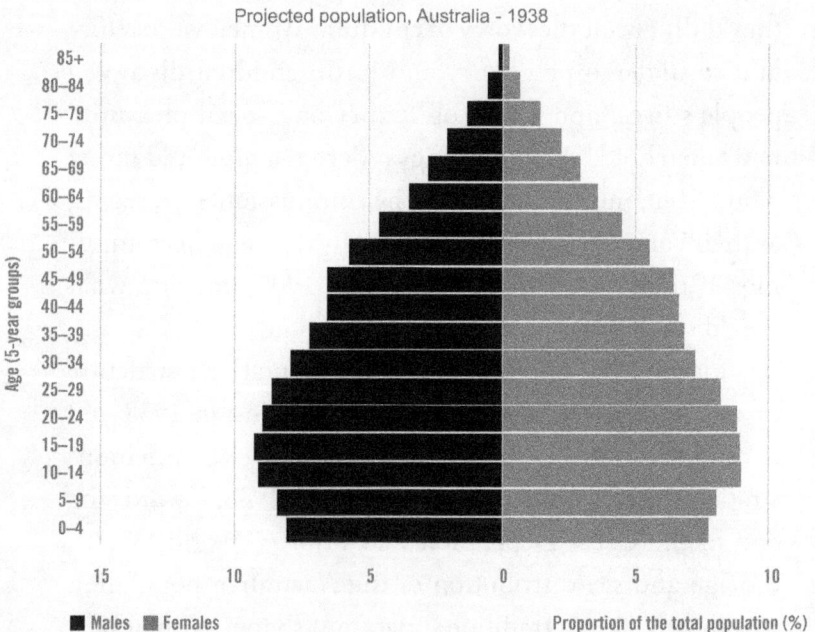

Age (5-year groups)

■ Males ■ Females

Proportion of the total population (%)

Modern demography

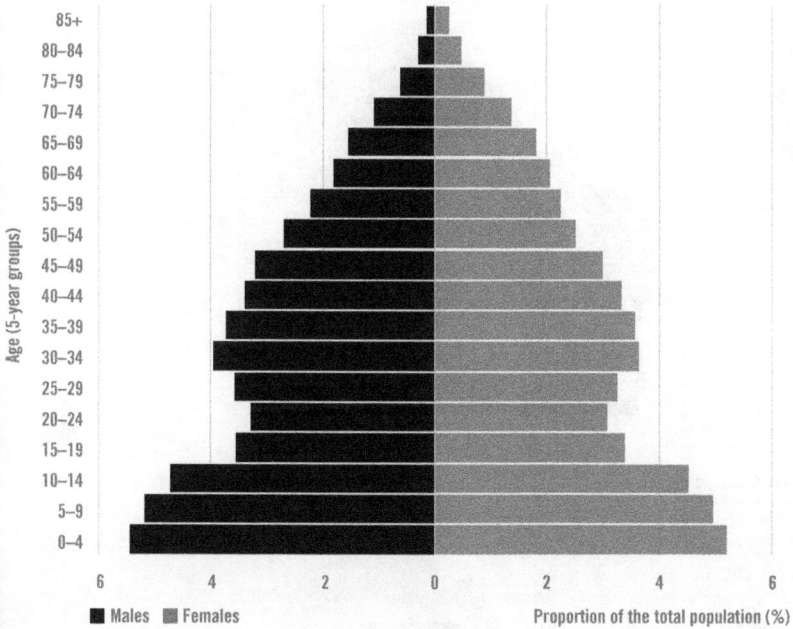

Projected population, Australia - 1958

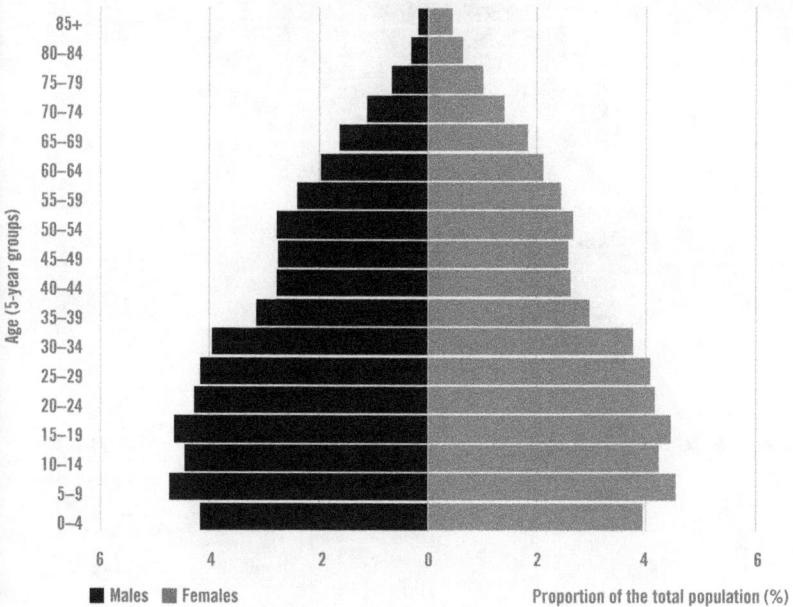

Projected population, Australia - 1978

The problem with us

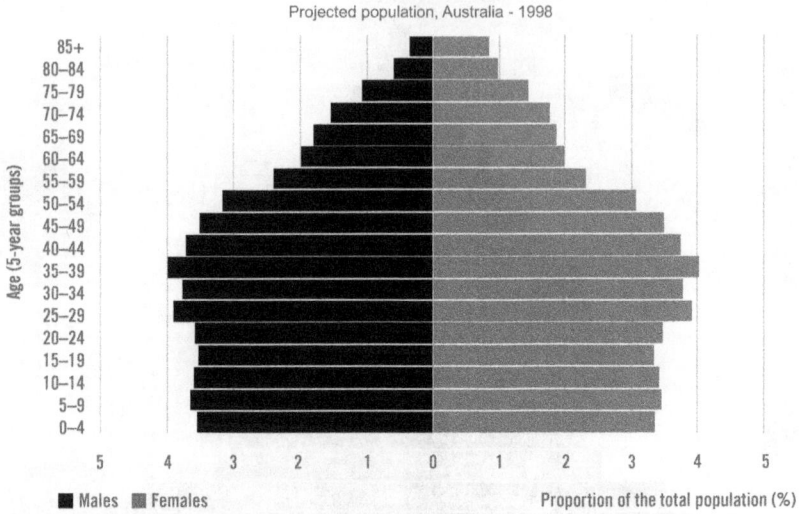

Projected population, Australia - 1998

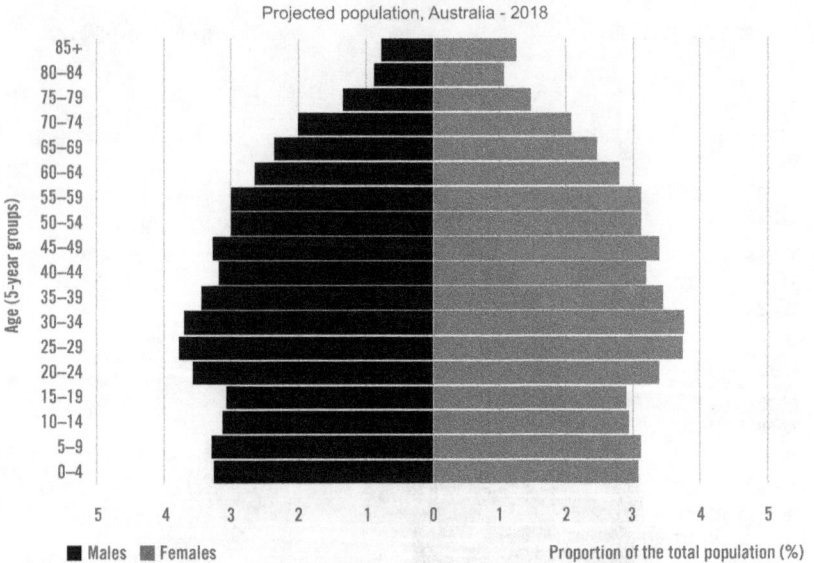

Projected population, Australia - 2018

Projected population, Australia - 2038

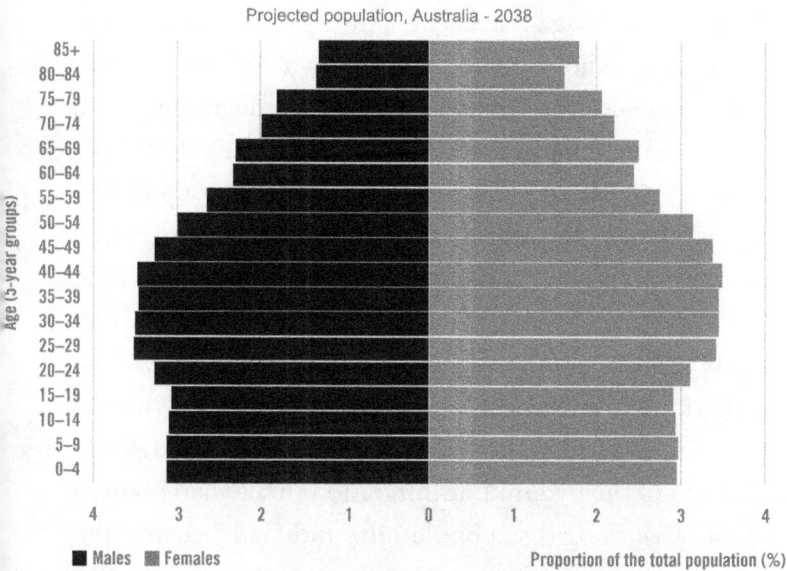

jumped after the war, and immigration intake was unprecedented. Postwar immigration contributed to the number of people in their peak working and reproductive years, and also to fertility, as migrants went on to have families in Australia. The first of the baby boomers were born, and the boom in births continued for almost a decade afterwards. The 1958 population pyramid depicts the early impact of the baby boom on the age structure of the Australian population. Population growth during this period was relatively high.

Fast-forward to 1978, and the age and sex distribution of Australia has changed. Growth rates were falling, but a younger median age reflects the fertility of the baby boomers, many of whom now had their own children. In the 40 years between the onset of war and the final throes of the disco age, Australia's population had more than doubled.

By 1998, the age structure was such that population ageing was clearly well on its way. Fertility had declined below replacement, overall growth rates were low, and the median population age was approaching mid-30s.

By 2018, population ageing was well and truly evident. Proportionally more people were aged 65 years and over, as the baby boomer cohort slowly made its way through life to the top of the pyramid. Immigration intake had boosted the early-working-age population, and had become the greatest contributor to population growth. Median age edged past the mid-30s, and the population ticked past the 25-million milestone.

It's projected that Australia's population will continue to grow in the future, albeit at a slower rate; that the median age will be pushed out to 40; and that ageing will become more pronounced as the tail of the boomer cohort rests at the top of the pyramid. The near-classic pyramid shape of 1938 will likely be replaced by a beehive shape.[8]

But what does all this ageing stuff really mean, and why does it matter?

Chief among the concerns associated with an ageing population is the increasing proportion of people over 65 to working-age people (15–65 years) and children (0–14 years). Why? Well, it comes down to money. The theory goes that working-aged people are more likely to be paying personal income tax, an important contributor to government coffers, whereas people below or past working age are less likely to be contributing to the pool of money necessary to support the population. While this is true, the way the debate is framed is often unnecessarily divisive. Young people are seen as having greater value to society, as they have more of their lives ahead of them during which to contribute. Older people, on the other hand, have already made their contribution to society, and now need its support. They are perceived as has-beens, past their prime. Like children, they are dependent and vulnerable – but unlike children, they supposedly have nothing further to give.

In discussions of population, the problem of supporting children and the elderly is often referred to as the 'dependency burden'. The dependency burden has serious demographic consequences, but the term itself has some pretty nasty connotations, which is why I prefer to call it the support ratio – I don't like the implication that children and older people are a drain on the economy. Young people haven't finished being educated yet, and older people have made and continue to make lifelong contributions to society. And what gives with the arbitrary 65-years-and-over cut-off? We all know that people work beyond that, in either paid or voluntary roles. Conversely, we all know that sometimes young people are a hell of a lot older than 15 before they get a job, even though they're technically eligible for employment at that age.

Whichever term you prefer, though, the data makes

it clear that there's an upward trend in the proportion of Australians aged over 65 years compared to the proportion aged between 15 and 64. This represents a break with the past. The total support ratio has fluctuated between 1938 and 2018, but children have always been its biggest component, until very recently. This is no surprise, given the sizable contributions the baby boomer cohort made to the total fertility rate of the postwar years. But as the number of children has decreased, the number of elderly people has increased markedly.

In 2018, there were 29 children aged below 15 years for every 100 working-age people, as opposed to 24 people aged 65 years or more. By 2038, it's expected older people will very slightly outnumber children: there will be 29 children and 30 older people for every 100 working-age people. This isn't necessarily a bad thing, but Australia hasn't been terribly good at managing such changes in the past. Policy approaches here have tended (and tend) to be more bandaid than reform. Preparedness is essential, but so far nothing much has been done. Attempts to increase the age at which Australians are eligible for the pension have been met with great frustration and opposition: imagine working most of your life, with an end goal in sight, only to have the goalposts moved as you get closer. This is particularly hurtful for people for whom physical labour has been their main source of employment, for people with disabilities, and for First Nations Australians, whose life expectancy is below the national average.

While most Australians can now expect to live into

FIGURE 3.3 Age-related support ratio in Australia per 100 people[9]

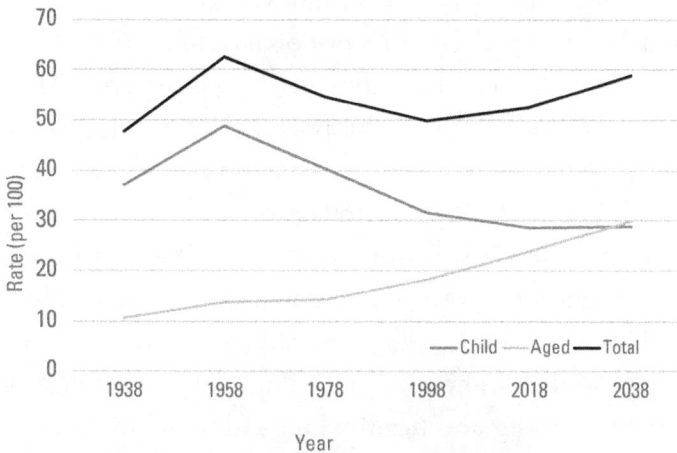

their 80s, meaning they'll be alive and eligible to claim the age pension for around 15 years after their retirement, this may not always be the case. Taking a pessimistic view, life expectancy might plateau and even decline. There's certainly evidence that obesity and sedentary lifestyles might see future generations live shorter lives than their parents and grandparents.[10] It's worth noting, too, that austerity is thought to be responsible for declining life expectancy in the United Kingdom and United States over the last ten years.[11] But adopting an optimistic view instead sets us on an interesting pathway. Think technological advancements that might delay the effects of ageing on the body and brain. (No, not quite like heads sloshing around in preservation jars perched atop robotic bodies, à la *The Simpsons* or *Futurama*. Or maybe a little like that?)

Let's revisit the concepts of life span and longevity, which I mentioned briefly back in Chapter 1. Life span is the theoretical age to which our bodies *could* survive, and longevity is the actual age to which we *do* survive.[12] Many have hypothesised about the potential span of a human life, some guessing that we might live anywhere from 120 to 140 years, or even to 160 years.

John Bongaarts, a world-renowned Dutch-American demographer, proposes that humans suffer from inbuilt obsolescence: our bodies start falling apart and repair is impossible.[13] There's no evolutionary advantage in remaining strong and healthy long after our children and grandchildren are grown up. Genes that affect our health during our biological prime tend to be weeded out of the population through natural selection, whereas genes that make us frail *after* we're done rearing children are passed on endlessly. Whether you have one, many or no children, you'll still start to fall apart: no one can escape this inbuilt obsolescence. Depressing, right? I long for the day the kids leave me an empty-nester and I have an abundance of time. But will the body hold up? Well, here's the main issue: population ageing is associated with people living longer, but it's also associated with greater morbidity due to previous diseases or injuries, and the sheer fact that living longer means greater exposure to risk of ill health. This is of great concern to those focused on the budget bottom line.

Economic success is often reduced to the three Ps: population, participation and productivity.[14] Population represents potential, because it makes participation and productivity possible. Participation refers to economic participation – taking part in the workforce – and productivity is the measure of how effective and efficient we are at work. The realities for Australia are this: female labour force participation has increased since the 1970s, but despite the commonly held belief that women hold the key to ensuring labour supply, there's a limit to how much further this can go. Without major policy reform, women's participation in paid work may not reach its potential, which could lead to greater gender inequality – a troubling idea, after several decades of significant progress on this front. Child care, gender equality at work (especially pay parity), and family-friendly workplaces are all essential if we're to keep moving towards the goal of full participation. And as for the third P, productivity has slowed and remains stable, while government spending has exceeded that gained through revenue.[15]

Concerns over health expenditure also plague policymakers and the financial boffins tasked with balancing the economy. The most recent available data on health expenditure broken down by age and sex has a similar distribution to the age-specific death rates we saw in the previous chapter. In infancy, age-specific health expenditure is around $2000 per person, before dropping to its lowest level between the ages of 5 and 14 (less than $1000 per person).[16] Up to the age of 54, the growth in expenditure per person steadily rises; for women, costs peak between 25 and 34 years of age, during their peak childbearing years. From the age of 45 onwards, the costs for men overtake those for women on a per capita basis. For those aged 55 and over, health expenditure per person escalates quite rapidly, until it reaches just over $14 000 for men and around $12 000 for woman aged 85 and over. By age 85, health expenditure per person is nearly 20 times higher than that for children between 5 and 14 years. This figure reflects the older population's higher incidence of disability and morbidity, which start to escalate at around 65 years of age. But while spending on health for older people might seem like cause for alarm, remember that health is cumulative, and the rung some of us start on is higher than others. Taking a preventative approach to health care could significantly redress inequality and at the same time bring down costs incurred later in life.

I've just presented the overall picture here, without delving into detail about subgroups within the Australian population known to suffer disparities in health. Among these subgroups are women, people from linguistically and culturally diverse backgrounds, First Nations Australians and people from socioeconomically disadvantaged backgrounds. It's vital to the nation's overall health that *all* Australians have easy access to the health care they require. Equity is key. And not just in older ages, but throughout life.

Australia's changing face

Migration is one way to help keep a population economically afloat. International overseas migration can help offset the adverse economic impacts associated with an ageing workforce and population – so long as it's demand-driven and skills-based, the two requirements that form the basis of the Australian scheme. But with international migration comes change and diversity, which can be challenging for some. Remember, much of the current Australian population was either raised during the time of the White Australia policy or raised by people who were – despite best efforts, a policy such as that one has lasting effects.

Migration in the post-White-Australia-policy era has been dominated by skills-based migration, yet there is a disproportionate focus on refugees and asylum seekers in our public discourse, particularly since the 1970s. Asylum seekers, referred to in the popular vernacular as boat people because of their mode of arrival, first started coming to Australia predominantly from East Timor, then from Vietnam, and then China. They haven't always been given a warm welcome by politicians or the public, but from the mid-1970s until the late 1990s those seeking refuge found it in Australia, figuratively and literally. Those who've arrived since, with the bulk of applications coming from the Middle East and the Indian subcontinent, have not been as readily welcomed. Public attitudes towards asylum seekers, shaped by events in 2001, have become less tolerant, even hostile. Australia's policy of mandatory detention and offshore processing of 'unauthorised arrivals' both feeds and is fed by this popular fear of people fleeing war and persecution. The actual number of asylum seekers coming here by boat is tiny, making very little contribution to overall migration.

The most recent population census showed that England, at 15 per cent, remained the number one country of birth for people in Australia born overseas.[17] New Zealand was second (8.4 per cent), closely followed by China (8.3 per cent). Also in the top five were India (7.4 per cent) and the Philippines (3.8 per cent). But this data hides the true change that migration is bringing. It tells us about the entire population born overseas, not just about more recent migrants, when it's recent patterns of migration that are most relevant here. The data tells us where people are coming from when they move to Australia, and it shows very clearly the changing face of the nation: we're a more diverse and multicultural community now than we were in the past. Indeed, there's been a changing of the guard: the white Europeans who were once the majority of migrants to Australia have been replaced by people from closer to home.

This is confronting for some Australians whose notion of Australia is white. They're usually white themselves; they grew up speaking English; and they are, if only nominally, Christian. These people don't tend to think of themselves as immigrants, or the descendants of immigrants, but of course they are. Even after more than 200 years in Australia, most white Australians remain ignorant of the richness and diversity of the First Nations cultures they live alongside. Few could tell you the name of an Indigenous language, let alone speak one fluently. Yet white Australians opposed to non-white immigration complain that non-European migrants don't assimilate. Regardless of this country's First Nations roots, many white Australians see any face that's not white and European as foreign.

Figure 3.4 shows the top-ten-ranking countries of birth represented in net overseas migration to Australia in the ten years from 2007, including both permanent and temporary migration. India and China consistently held

FIGURE 3.4 Net overseas migration 'top ten' by country of birth, Australia, 2007–2008 and 2017–2018[18]

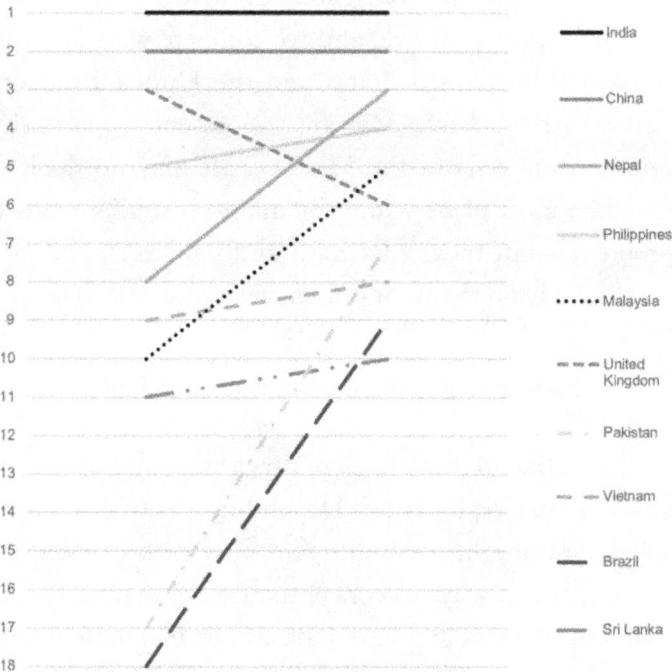

the top two places throughout this period. Nepal, formerly in eighth position, took out third spot at the end of the ten years. Moving from fourth to fifth position was the Philippines, while Malaysia moved from tenth to fifth. India, China, Nepal, the Philippines and Malaysia were the top five countries contributing to net overseas migration in Australia in 2007 – none of them white, none of them English-speaking. What of the United Kingdom? Well, it fell from third to sixth place. But take a look at Pakistan's trajectory – now *that* is a country to pay attention to.

Australia isn't the only country in the world needing immigrants to survive, and we compete with the likes of Canada, the United States and the United Kingdom to attract them here. Migrants represent opportunity. Migrants from Asia or the Middle East may not look or sound like most of us – and for many Australians this is a problem – but they work hard and pay taxes, and as a nation we rely on them for our survival.

Inequality and the Bank of Mum and Dad

Australians like to think this country is the land of the fair go, but is that really true? Depending on which expert you ask, you might get a different answer, because there are a number of ways to conceptualise inequality. Two of the measures demographers look at are income equality and wealth inequality – the money coming in every week or every month as opposed to the savings, investments or assets you have accumulated and can draw on at will.

Overall, wealth inequality is growing, fuelled, at least in part, by Australia's demography. To illustrate, let's consider the humble home.

Ask anyone in Australia, especially anyone over 50, about the quintessential Australian dream. They might tell you it's owning a piece of this place: a home. But for many younger Australians, that quintessential Australian dream is so way out of sight, it's a sinking ship off the very far horizon. This matters, because homeownership is an important contributor to wealth in Australia. Homes account for almost half of household wealth among owner-occupiers. Owning your home also provides benefits above and beyond a secure, stable place to live. For example, Australians faced with financial hardship can gain early access to superannuation savings to avoid losing their home – if they *own* that home. Renters in the same situation are not permitted to draw on their superannuation to pay rent. In other words, faced with the loss of their home, owners are given a get-out-of-the-crap-free card. Meanwhile, non-homeowners are stiffed, given a choice between homelessness or bankruptcy. All due to the home, or lack thereof. Other benefits of homeownership include financial equity in the home, potentially enabling you to buy another property as investment, start your own business or help your adult children get into the housing market – all of which would be much more difficult for renters.

If you own your home, I imagine you might be thinking, 'I saved and worked hard for my home.' Perhaps you did, but remember that ladder of opportunity. Some of us

FIGURE 3.5 Homeownership rates among individuals
aged 18 and over, 2002–2014[19]

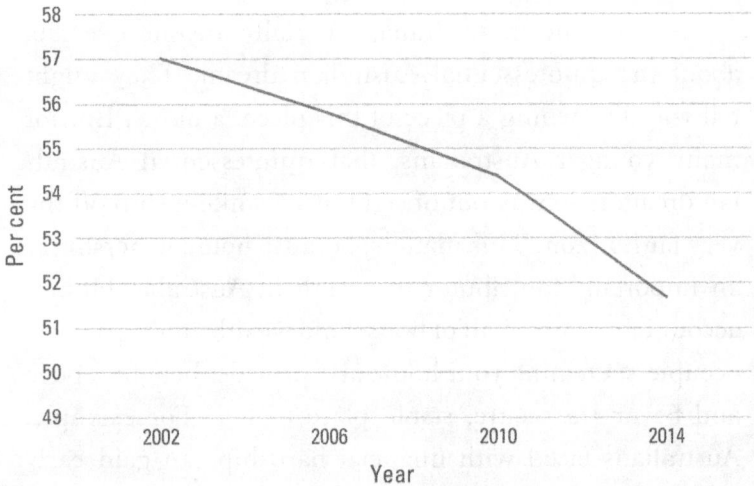

work hard but just never get that chance. Others may enjoy the benefits of homeownership without doing much – or anything at all – to earn it. It's the ovarian lottery, rather than hard work, that allows people to get ahead in life. And this is indeed what we're seeing in Australia now.

Homeownership has declined since 2002, based on data from the national survey of Housing, Income and Labour Dynamics in Australia. Figure 3.5 uses this data to show the hefty decline (5.3 percentage points) in overall homeownership rates between 2002 and 2014.

When we break these figures down by age group, one particular trend stands out: younger people have experienced a much higher decline in homeownership than

FIGURE 3.6 Homeownership rates by age group, 2002–2014[20]

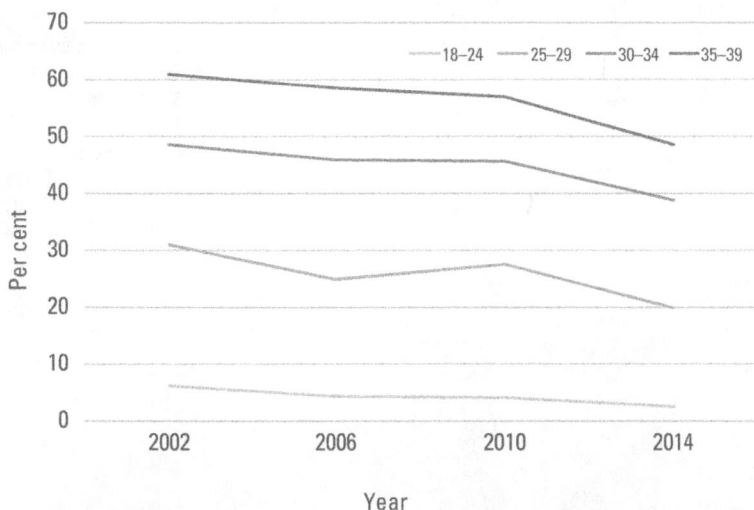

older cohorts, with an overall decline of almost 11 percent-age points for those aged under 40. Figure 3.6 provides a closer look at the younger age groups. Most concerning is the downward trend in homeownership among those aged between 35 and 39, the stage of life during which we might expect people to have families and be looking to settle and establish roots. Between 2002 and 2014, homeownership among this age group fell by nearly 13 percentage points. And it's not because people are buying homes at younger ages: the decline is seen across all younger age groups.

Figure 3.7 depicts the rate of homeownership according to family type for adults under 40. Couples with children have seen the greatest decline in homeownership of

FIGURE 3.7 Homeownership rates, 18–39 years, by family type, 2002–2014[21]

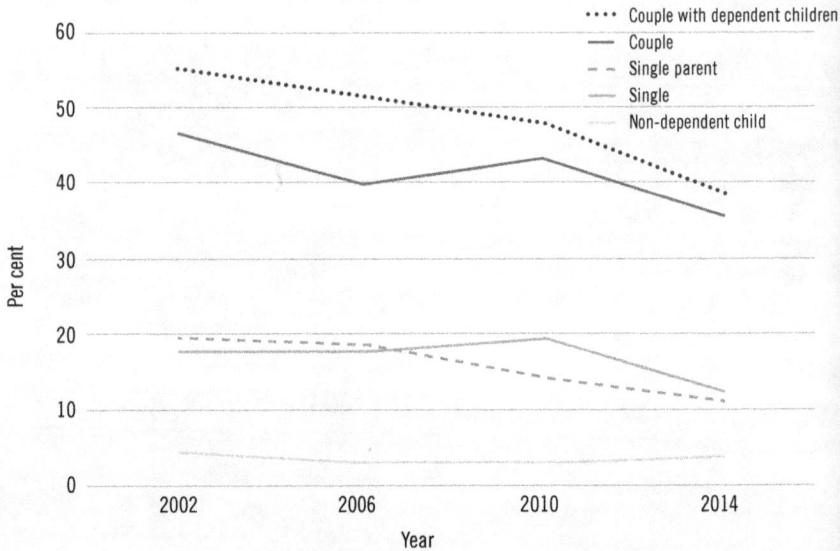

all the family types examined, experiencing a massive drop of nearly 17 percentage points between 2002 and 2014. The majority of all young couples with children live in rented housing. This means they are vulnerable to eviction, less likely to be able to save, and don't enjoy the freedom home-owners have to make a house truly one's home.

Once again, our family background plays a big part, determining whether we'll rent or buy. But what do Mum and Dad have to do with it? The so-called Bank of Mum and Dad is the ninth biggest lender in Australia, based on loan stock ($29.4 billion). In total, 60 per cent of first homebuyers were helped by the Bank of Mum and Dad in 2018.[22] That's a lot. This isn't parents dying and leaving inheritances. This is live parents helping their adult children get into the housing market. Put another way, the majority of first home buyers are only able to enter the housing market because of the wealth of their parents.

Tightening regulation has seen the rate of parental support drop to 20 per cent in 2019. This might be good for parents, relieved of the financial pressure of supporting their adult children. But think of the kids and the grandkids, without anyone to give them a leg-up in a housing market the likes of which Australia has never seen before. No doubt the Bank of Mum and Dad will find other ways of helping kids – people with financial means have the capacity to find smart workarounds and take advantage of loopholes in the system.

Tax incentives offered to property investors in Australia are a big part of the problem, particularly negative gearing. We're at the point now where people are paying income tax to help fund investors who own multiple properties while young people are stuck paying rent to those same investors and living in insecure housing. This system has contributed to a perverse situation in which young people find themselves awaiting the death of their parents, hoping like hell they don't spend the inheritance funding their retirement activities. But with Australians living longer than ever, they might be waiting a lot longer than they're anticipating. Will this mean that young people put off having children until later in life? Is the baby boom that got us into this predicament now the cause of a baby bust? Weirdly, this baby bust could mean even more pressure on government coffers and greater stress on the rapidly shrinking working-age population. Think it's hard to crack into the housing market for first home buyers now? Wait a little bit ... if nothing changes, it's going to get much worse.

The point is that wealth inequality matters. According to the latest data, the top 20 per cent of Australian households own the majority of total wealth (63 per cent). Meanwhile, the bottom 20 per cent of Australian households own less than 1 per cent of all wealth. Yes, 1 per cent.

Property ownership is responsible for the size of this disparity. It is property ownership that has boosted the fortunes of middle-wealth and high-wealth households in Australia, and it is the lack of property ownership causing the financial stagnation of low-wealth households. Wealth inequality driven by property ownership is fracturing society. Young people face a bleak economic future, one in which they may not share the spoils previous generations have accumulated. The question we must again ask ourselves is this: do we want luck to determine success? Or hard work?

*

In short, Australia's demography presents a challenge. Population growth is slowing and inequality is growing. Successive governments have opted to slap a bandaid on these problems, at best, rather than confront the issues.

The 'intergenerational bargain' is a tricky one to negotiate, and there are no easy answers – but our nation's future is at stake.

International migration has played a vital part in bolstering Australia's economy, especially via its important contribution to a shrinking workforce. Our growing diversity is a strength, giving us an edge in the global marketplace. But for some, the changing face of Australia is a frightening prospect. The result of their distrust and suspicion is conflict, aggression and social division. This fear cannot be allowed to fester. Instead of feeding intolerance, our leaders should promote not just tolerance but inclusivity, welcoming migrants into our community rather than demonising them. This is true even if we set aside moral questions and, instead, focus purely on self-interest. It's a simple fact: we can't survive without migration.

Our leaders also have to take decisive action against the rising threat to our national wellbeing posed by intergenerational wealth inequality. It's not a slow-burning issue. It's here and it's growing. Policy can and must be used to ensure that achieving financial security isn't an accident of birth, mostly a matter of luck, rather than hard work. Homeownership is just the tip of the iceberg. Whether or not it remains a vital aspect of wealth, one thing is for sure: while the core issues of today and tomorrow are clear, governments of all stripes choose to focus on matters of irrelevancy. Political point scoring is undermining our future.

CHAPTER 4

Population panic

It's hard to deny that population has become a great source of concern. Not a week goes by that a story in the media somewhere in Australia doesn't describe population as exploding, booming, deleterious or insufficient in some way. Kids are being crammed into classrooms, they say; trains don't run on time; roads are packed; high-rise buildings are popping up like termite mounds and blocking the sun; infrastructure is cracking and crumbling; families are being pushed to the fringes of towns and cities; people are sprawling uncontrollably everywhere ... Arrrgh. Population! The Ponzi scheme of perpetual growth is strangling our livelihoods and robbing us of our Australian birthrights. These are actual things said in media reports, on blogs, on the radio, on TV talk shows and on social media. The level of hysteria is palpable. Believe me. I've had hate pieces written about me, received death threats, been mailed violent racist manifestos (complete with decades-old newspaper clippings), and been the subject of some nasty personal attacks. Why? Because I talk population. But more importantly, I talk immigration. I talk about the advantages immigration brings to the nation.

The people most concerned about this appear to be white, male and privileged.

In public discourse, population has become code for immigration. When people say they're concerned about population, they usually mean they're concerned about the population growing due to immigration. Yet regardless of where you stand on the question of population size – whether you're worried about too much growth or not enough – the discussion has become so charged that even among reasonable people it doesn't take much for arguments to erupt about what size Australia should be. The media give a voice to those with simplistic, sensationalist views on the matter. And politicians love it. Alarmist sound bites and slogans grab our attention, with little regard for the truth or even plausibility. *Chinese-born population could exceed English-born population in Australia ...Migration surge risks support for welfare ... A population crush is pushing up Australian house prices ... Sydney trains buckle under immigration crush ... Melbourne's population explosion threatens to create a 'Bangkok situation' ...* These are the sorts of headlines we see constantly. If recent far-right protests and the success of conservative nationalist political parties are anything to go by, Australians are (like many people across the world) ripe for persuasion and exploitation by populist demagogues preaching fear. Fear that locals will no longer get a 'fair go' – locals, in this scenario, meaning Australian-born white people and sometimes migrants who are already here and want to 'shut the door behind them'.

Panic over population size, growth, distribution and composition has become a staple of popular and political discourse. We have an unhealthy fascination with the details: everything from how many children couples are having (or not having), to the cultural backgrounds of people having children. All of this has somehow become open for public debate. And, you guessed it, women and minority groups cop the worst of it.

Population panic in itself isn't necessarily anything to be worried about. Panic, after all, prompts action. Well, panic *can* prompt action, but sometimes it just results in tears, flailing arms and the impulse to turn and flee. The problem is that this panic isn't being used productively. Instead, it's being used to foment division and opposition, potentially fuelling hate. We've seen this happen in Australia in recent times. The creation of the myth of African gangs terrorising Australia's major cities is just one example of how unchecked panic can be transformed via political narrative into fear and hate.

Fear and growth

Population growth – upward or downward – hasn't typically been a mainstream concern in modern-day Australia, not since the postwar years … until the last ten years or so, that is. Some regional areas have experienced population declines and will continue to do so, but Australia's overall population isn't in decline. I mentioned in Chapter 2 that this was a problem facing Italy and South

Korea, but there are other countries facing population decline too, including Germany, Greece, Japan and
Russia. In the case of Germany, Japan and South Korea,
immigration has been recognised by government as their
ticket out of this demographic dilemma. For Australia,
though, growth has emerged as a deep concern: we have
an unhealthy focus on the size of our annual population
growth. Why? Because this population growth is fuelled
by immigration.

Immigration overtook natural increase as Australia's
largest source of population growth in 2005. Until then,
growth didn't rate as a concern. Natural increase results
from local births, babies born to local Australians. There's
nothing threatening about a newborn baby who'll be raised
in an Australian family. Immigration, on the other hand, is
the introduction of strangers – adult strangers, and sometimes their families – into the local community. Foreigners
represent the 'other', unfamiliar by definition. Those who
oppose immigration often fear competition from the other;
they want to reserve local resources for local people, and
resent the idea of having to share with those they see as
strangers.

No one likes being called a racist, though, so instead
of railing against immigration, politicians and others
warn against too-rapid growth. Pauline Hanson, leader
of the One Nation party, famously commented in 2018
that Australia's rate of population growth was the highest in the world.[1] Australia's growth is not fastest in the
world or even among OECD countries. Hanson and

similar-minded politicians have intimated and even outright stated that Australia is changing so much that white European Australians will soon become a minority. Claims that white (and non-Muslim) Australians are set to become a minority have been disproven, yet the fear persists.[2]

The reason it persists, of course, is that it's actively promoted. The promotion of such views has typically come from the fringes of Australian politics, but the voices of extremists have grown louder and more insistent since the 1990s, when Pauline Hanson first arrived on the political scene. The influence of these voices on the major parties is undeniable, which has only encouraged them to speak more loudly and express views that are even more extreme.

Former Queensland senator Fraser Anning is one such voice. Anning ran for the senate in 2016 as a member of One Nation, his name appearing third on the ticket. He received only 19 direct votes, but entered the senate in 2017 after his more successful colleague, Malcolm Roberts, was removed, ineligible due to dual Australian and foreign citizenship. (Oh, the irony.)[3] Having had a falling-out with Pauline Hanson in the meantime, Anning sat in the senate as an independent. He later joined Katter's Australia Party, but his extremist views on immigration saw him expelled only months later, at which point he became an independent again, free to peddle his own personal brand of far-right nationalism, and eventually established his own party, bearing his name.

Throughout his time in parliament, Anning frequently spoke of the 'hidden and disenfranchised', as though he was the second coming. The senator-by-default made quite the name for himself when it came to sparking population panic. Anning became known for his association with far-right groups and attendance at neo-Nazi events, and for calling for a return to the White Australia policy. He even went so far as calling for a plebiscite in which Australians could vote on whether immigration should only come from European countries – in his maiden speech to the senate, no less.[4] Anning is remembered for all this … and for being smashed in the head with an egg in the lead-up to the 2019 election.[5] Voters rejected Anning's brand of nativist populism in heartening fashion, booting him from the senate, but while he may have been a fringe politician, he garnered a huge amount of media attention along the way.

Fraser Anning seems to have disappeared, at least for the time being, but others in the anti-immigration movement have greater staying power. Pauline Hanson is possibly Australia's most successful far-right politician. The former fast-food shop owner used the same *I-am-the-people, I-speak-for-you* brand of politics as Anning, but she has used it more successfully and for far longer. Hanson warned of the perils of an 'Asian invasion' in the 1990s when she first arrived on the political scene. Upon her political revival in 2016, Hanson warned of a 'Muslim invasion'. She said that Australians were being 'swamped'. But when Hanson talks about Australians, what she really means is white people like her. She's not a fan of First Nations peoples claiming rights to their land. It was Hanson's controversial comments about Indigenous Australians that led to her being disendorsed by the Liberal party after she'd been added to the party ticket for the 1996 federal election.[6] It was too late to take her name off the ballot, and she won the seat and entered parliament as an independent. It's a story not unlike Anning's.

One thing is certain: Hanson seems afraid of white people losing their dominance over others. This is evidenced by Hanson's infamous motion, put to the senate in 2018, that it was 'OK to be white'. Others in the senate recognised this as a tagline used by far-right white supremacist movements, and fortunately the motion was defeated, 31 votes to 28.[7] The reason the motion was particularly controversial, though, was that government senators voted in favour of it – not realising, the Liberal party insisted later, that they were endorsing a racist slogan. Then-senator Derryn Hinch stated during the debate that Anning and Hanson were competing to outdo each other in racism, and that the upcoming federal election was the motivator. Hanson also called for a plebiscite on immigration intake in 2018, suggesting that the Australian public should have a say about the size of the immigration program. That motion was also quashed, but more effectively.

Elections since 2001 have certainly been racially charged. The far-right talk about 'protecting' Australians and 'putting Australia first', to rally the people to their cause. In reality, though, they are trying to scare people, using fear to motivate them. Politicians try to outdo each other in their 'tough on borders' stance. In the lead-up to the 2019 federal election, the leaders of the two major parties, Labor's Bill Shorten and the now prime minster, Scott Morrison of the Liberal party, each framed population (in other words, immigration) as a problem requiring remedy. Shorten, with the support of the secretary of the Australian Council of Trade Unions, Sally McManus, suggested migrants were taking local jobs. The problem, as Shorten described it, was that temporary migrants were undercutting local workers' wages and robbing them of employment opportunities. Shorten even went so far as adopting an Australians-first rhetoric concerning education and training in his 2019 budget reply speech in parliament:

> We already know the expertise our nation will need in the next decade ... I don't want Australia to meet these needs with skills visas, I want to train our people for these jobs. There is no excuse for a skills vacancy to last one day longer than it takes to train an Australian to do that job ... So instead of looking overseas or relying on temporary visas, employers will have a skilled local workforce ready to go.[8]

These sentiments weren't new: similar thinking informed Labor's 'Australians First' video, produced in 2017, promoting employment priority for Australians and depicting only white people.[9]

Of course we want Australians to be trained in skills that allow them to participate in the workforce. But the problem remains that the local population is either not interested or not sufficiently skilled to undertake the kinds of jobs that have historically appeared on the skills shortage list, including meat worker, chef, hairdresser and accountant. The reality is that migrants are necessary to help make up these skill shortages. Training for the local population is a vital component of a comprehensive population policy, but the trouble is that adopting such rhetoric – *Australians first* – ignores what's actually happening. There has been a growing preference among school leavers and employers for higher education over vocational training.[10] Vocational education, namely TAFE, has been underfunded over the long term, undermining its potential as an option instead of university. Additionally, Australia lacks the sheer numbers needed to fill job vacancies, due to the ageing population. Without immigration, Australian labour supply growth would almost be zero.[11] (More on that in the next chapter.) Saying 'Australians first' just primes the public for other anti-migrant sentiments, but it's an effective political strategy.

Morrison's team talked 'congestion busting', and continues to do so. Congestion busting is thinly veiled code for cutting immigration, a euphemism blaming migrants for our problems. Time spent in traffic, public transport not running on time or being persistently crowded, packed classrooms and run-down schools, unaffordable housing – all of these issues, and more, are put down to overpopulation. The message is: *We're full.* As a consequence, Morrison's government cut our permanent migration intake for 2019–2020 from 190 000 to 160 000, pushing more and more people into a state of limbo, leaving them to wait, on bridging visas, for longer and longer periods while their application for permanency is delayed to fudge the figures. With most of these people already here in the community, the cut was an empty gesture that couldn't conceivably address 'congestion' in any way.

Some applicants for permanent residency spend years on a bridging visa. During that time, they contribute to Australian society and pay tax. While they wait for their applications to be approved or denied, many have to put their lives on hold. Forming relationships and having children – these things wait. They wait for as long as it takes for their application to be reviewed, potentially up to two years.[12] Meanwhile, the non-refundable $8000 fee for residency is pocketed and spent by the Australian government. Imagine living in a country for years, all the while waiting to hear whether or not you can stay. Migrants are people willing to take a punt on Australia and its people, and we owe them more than this. They're ready to totally uproot their lives, to travel to a new place, contribute to a new country and establish entirely new relationships. Yet subsequent governments in Australia have held out one hand to take their money and skills and then slapped them with the other, endorsing and promoting public feelings of resentment and hostility towards them. Sounds like an abusive relationship to me.

To give you some idea of how useless and symbolic a gesture it was to cut the immigration intake by 30 000 people, we only need to look at the difference between the annual permanent migrant intake, with its new ceiling of 160 000 immigrants, and the *actual* increase in the population, otherwise known as net overseas migration, which in the 2017–2018 financial year was 238 200 people. The net overseas migration figure, as you may remember from Chapter 2, takes into account not just permanent migration but also temporary migration. There were in fact 527 600 migrant arrivals that year – fewer than in the previous year – of whom only around 90 000 held permanent visas. There were also 289 300 migrant *departures*, which the Australian Bureau of Statistics notes is the highest number on record. What this demonstrates is that cutting the permanent migrant intake is really just fiddling with one part of the equation, and doesn't necessarily mean a cut to overall population. In any case, the permanent intake has already been declining for a number of years, hovering around 160 000, even before the official cut. Fortunately for all of us, net overseas migration figures have remained quite strong. Governments have been playing a game of smoke and mirrors: first creating the illusion that population is the cause of our problems, then 'solving' it through cuts to immigration that don't have any real effect. Our leaders know that we rely on immigration to survive, but they're reluctant to acknowledge that publicly. Instead, they spin us a line, trying to look as though they're acting when in fact they're doing nothing at all, and demonising migrants as they do so.

Talk of congestion busting avoids the real heart of the issue: Australia's planning and infrastructure has been inadequate for far too long. We're paying the price already, but it's set to worsen.[13] Trouble is, we haven't invested in ourselves. Aside from the money needed to build, maintain and update infrastructure, the time it takes to do the actual building typically exceeds Australian electoral terms. Three or four years is just not enough for a project that, done properly, could take 20 years or more. The Snowy Mountains scheme is an example of the kind of long-term project we don't see anymore. We also need migrants to help build the stuff: roads, housing and all that.

Infrastructure in Australia's biggest city, Sydney, was poorly resourced for nearly two decades under the leadership of Labor premier Bob Carr.[14] Carr's approach to infrastructure and population growth was: *If you don't build it, they won't come.* He drew heavily on the late-1960s doomsday philosophy espoused by Paul Ehrlich, American biologist and author of *The Population Bomb*.[15] Ehrlich famously predicted the downfall of humankind through overpopulation, though his prediction has not yet come to pass. Carr claimed in 2000: 'Sydney is full'. Australian economist Saul Eslake, scathing of Carr's approach to immigration and population matters, said in 2006 that many of New South Wales' economic woes had been 'self-inflicted by the policy mistakes of the government led for a decade by Bob Carr'.[16] Eslake felt that Carr's public commentary concerning immigration had undermined public confidence in the economy of the state. We're still playing catch-up as a result of this arrogant short-sightedness, and the hurt it has caused is felt far beyond Sydney, and even beyond New South Wales.

Government short-termism has reduced political cycles to a year or six months. It's about getting wins, scores on the board. This is seen both in general policy and infrastructure development. Getting elected seems more important to some of our politicians than what they are able to do with power once they've secured it. This populist approach to politics and policy across the federal, state and even local levels of government gets in the way of the kind of long-term investment required to finance major reform and development.

This is perhaps best illustrated by the handling of the national infrastructure plan released in 2011. In the aftermath of the Sustainable Population Strategy for Australia inquiry, the Department of Infrastructure and Transport launched a new national urban policy.[17] The minister responsible was Anthony Albanese, who would go on to be leader of the opposition after the Coalition victory at the 2019 federal election. The new urban policy laid out a road map of sorts for the future of Australian towns and cities. It was ambitious, setting out a long-term plan. The report was evidence-based, apolitical and optimistic about the future awaiting the nation. The main problem was that the goals outlined in the report had not been allocated funding. But it was – and remains – the best attempt at long-term planning Australia had seen in many years, possibly since the postwar rebuilding of the nation. It was to be very short lived. When the Labor government was voted out in 2013, so too was its long-term vision for Australian infrastructure, ushering in an era in which fears of growth dictate policy. Governments at all levels now point the finger at migrants, blaming them for problems they haven't caused, rather than dealing with the actual problem, that of inadequate infrastructure.

Our leaders should know better, but many individual Australians don't. For many, the fear of population growth stems from their own experience of inequality, lived or perceived. Migrants are blamed for rising housing prices and the inability of first home buyers to break into the market, when the true cause of this problem, as we've seen, is an ageing population and an unfair system of tax incentives for property investors.

The perception that migrants are taking economic opportunities away from locals is based on what people see around them – they're just interpreting what they see incorrectly, because they're not in possession of all the facts. Perception is more powerful than reality, and we base our behaviour on what we think we see, not necessarily what we're actually seeing. Crime is a great example of this. If we believe crime to be high or rising in our local area, we might not allow our children to play outside; we might restrict walking, and avoid being outside during particular times of the day; we might feel frightened and anxious. Our perceptions of crime are better predictors of our beliefs and behaviours than the actual crime rates for the area we live in. The public tends to fear crime far more than necessary.

Our perception of migrants may be equally inaccurate. Despite Australia's high migrant population, many of us don't encounter newly arrived migrants in our family and social circles, instead forming opinions based on what we observe of them in the local community and in the workplace. But forming opinions based on what we see can be dangerous, if we don't know the full story. You might, for example, see a newly arrived migrant moving into a beautiful house on your street, driving the latest model of car, or wearing nice clothing, and jump to the conclusion that migrants are being better provided for than locals. But here's the thing. People who migrate to Australia pay substantial amounts of money for the privilege – around $8000 just to lodge an application for permanent residency – and they must also prove they can pay for their own health care and education, and that of any children they have. Australia doesn't permit non-permanent migrants to draw on social security, Medicare or public education: no free anything. This is despite the fact that migrants pay Australian tax. The government pockets their money without any concern for timely processing of applications. In short, it's not cheap to migrate, meaning that migrants are on average more affluent than the local Australian population, but they're not being given a leg-up over anyone else. If anything, they're giving the country a leg-up, contributing higher individual income tax on average than locals – but the myths persist.[18]

Population, policy and immigration threats

Looking at the growth of the Australian population since 1901, it's clear that the total estimated resident population

FIGURE 4.1 Population size and growth rate, Australia, 1901–2018[19]

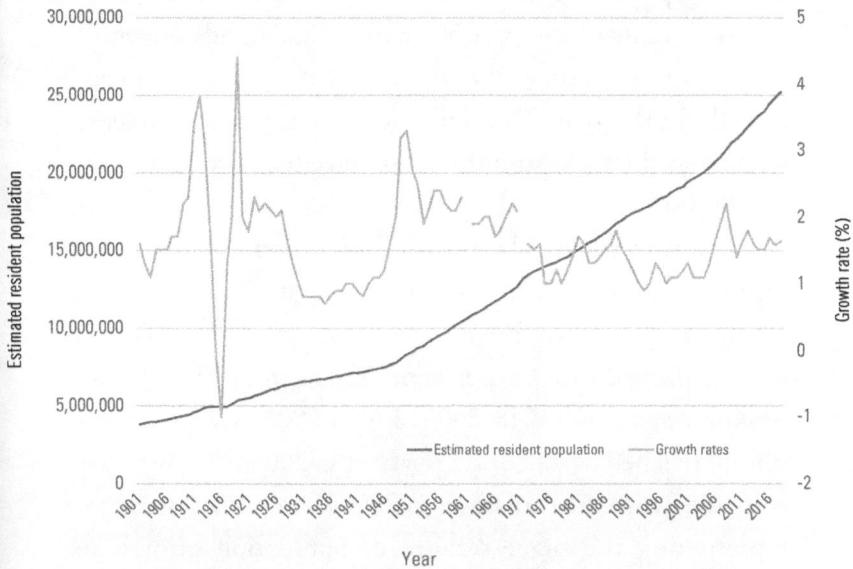

NOTE Data do not include accurate Indigenous population figures until 1971, and Indigenous births have only been recorded since 1966. Breaks in the line represent gaps in the trend data.

has seen a steady and sustained increase. This is no co-incidence, and no mistake: population growth has been vital to Australia's economic prosperity.

Figure 4.1 shows the number of people in Australia climbing from around 4 million at Federation to around 25 million in 2018. The population over time is represented by the dark line, which has a straightforward upward trajectory. The growth rate, on the other hand, represented by the lighter line, has fluctuated substantially over the past century, due to differences in the year-on-year changes in magnitude. Since the 1970s, annual population growth has blipped up and down, not surprising given the sociodemographic events of the past 50 years. What stands out most in recent years is the spike in 2008, peaking at 2.2 per cent growth for the year. This spike sticks out. But the increase leading to the spike and the rates since tell an equally fascinating story.

Following John Howard's intimation in 2001 that immigration – particularly the immigration of people of Islamic faith – was a threat to national security, population growth dropped to 1.1 per cent. Then, in 2005, it began to climb again – 1.3 in 2005, 1.6 in 2006, 1.9 in 2007 – until it reached a peak of 2.2 per cent in 2008. This increase coincided with the transition in 2005 from natural increase representing the biggest share of population growth to net overseas migration. This was despite federal treasurer Peter Costello's call to the nation to procreate, which, as we discussed in Chapter 2, had absolutely no effect. The climb down from the 2008 peak occurred at the same time as the global financial crisis, which Australia was somewhat protected from by the actions of the Labor government of the day. From the 2.2 per cent high, population growth dropped to 1.8 in 2009 and then to 1.4 per cent in 2010.

Population projections released by the Australian Bureau of Statistics in 2008 had Australia's population reaching 35.5 million people by 2056.[20] Kevin Rudd was all in favour of this growth, openly welcoming this potential future population. But when the Intergenerational Report was published by the Department of the Treasury in 2009, it calculated that Australia would reach 35.9 million people by 2050, earlier than projected by the ABS.[21] A bigger population, coming sooner than expected. The crap hit the fan. Rudd remained committed to his so-called big Australia – until it became clear that the general public didn't agree. The issue exploded, both in the media and the community. Politicians in particular had a great amount to say on the matter. Rudd's own party colleagues were running scared, and called for brakes on population. This is the paradox of how immigration is portrayed in Australia: one day it's touted as economic manna from heaven, and the next it's seen as a threat to the nation's wellbeing.

As it turned out, Treasury had assumed a higher fertility rate than the Australian Bureau of Statistics had. Projections are only as good as the assumptions they're based on, and our assumptions about fertility, mortality and migration can never be absolutely certain. It's kind of like trying to predict what a toddler is going to do based on their past behaviour – there are too many variables to consider, not all of which are observable. But this simple explanation couldn't cut through the resulting media storm, or the public hand-wringing. It was on, as they say, like Donkey Kong. Within months of the publication of the Intergenerational Report, a minister was appointed to the newly created portfolio of population. Tony Burke had the honour of being Australia's first minister for population. As a demographer, my little heart sang. Finally population was getting its rightful attention, even if it was for the wrong reasons. Rudd then called a population inquiry in 2010, largely to appease concerns raised following his welcoming of a big Australia.

The inquiry was a significant undertaking, lasting a year and involving wide stakeholder engagement, expert advisory panels and public consultation, and finishing with the tabling of a lengthy report.[22] The report set out a framework for an economically sustainable population, with a focus on suburban jobs, sustainable regional development and promoting regional living. Skill shortages, labour force participation, the effectiveness of the migration program, infrastructure and regional investment were also discussed. But no population target was set, despite the brouhaha over how big Australia should be, and before the inquiry's report was even released, Rudd had been ousted by his deputy, Julia Gillard, who didn't share her predecessor's enthusiasm for a big Australia.[23] It was the most comprehensive inquiry into population Australia has seen, and it laid out the need for a broad and encompassing policy approach, yet it ultimately had very little effect. Immigration and borders continued – and continue – to take central place in the political narrative.

Cutting immigration, stopping boats, interning asylum seekers in offshore camps: all of these things show us that Australia's problem accepting 'the other' didn't end with the White Australia policy. In Chapter 1, I talked about the history of this policy, which assumed that white Europeans were somehow superior to other people and which therefore sought to limit immigration to Australia by those from any other background. Though the policy came to an end in 1975, and our immigration policy is now officially non-discriminatory, the White Australia mentality still lingers. In theory, we no longer privilege white people over others, but we still discriminate in favour of English-speakers by including language requirements among the eligibility criteria. Funnily enough, many Australians might not meet the English requirements that many migrants are expected to.

But have our attitudes evolved at all? And if so, how are they changing? Public opinion, especially when measured over time, offers powerful insight into these questions, showing us Australia's changing view of immigration and the expectations locals have of migrants. The proportion of people in Australia who believe that immigration intake is too high or too low is fluctuating, according to a survey of thousands of Australians by independent think tank the Lowy Institute (see Figure 4.2). But since 2017, the proportion of Australians reporting immigration was too high has outstripped those who say it is about right or too low. This proportion peaked in 2018, when more than 50 per cent of people reported that immigration was too high.

We often hear that populism is on the rise, and that politicians just respond to what electors want. My take on it, based on the data, is that politicians can't blame the public: they are actively driving anti-immigration sentiment themselves, not simply reacting to it. What's the evidence? Well, opinion towards immigration intake in 2014 and 2017 was quite favourable, with a majority of Australians saying immigration levels were just right or too low.

FIGURE 4.2 Public opinion on immigration intake, Australia, 2014 and 2017–2019[24]

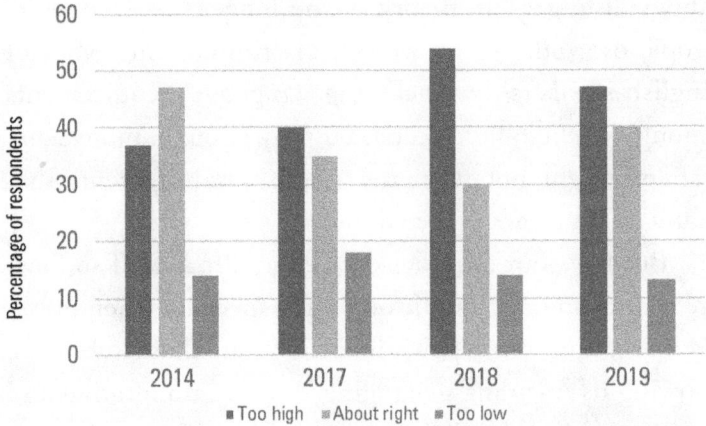

Immigration and population weren't the focus of political debate in either of those years. I'd also point out that net overseas migration remained at roughly the same level between 2017 and 2018, and yet in 2018, when immigration and population had become the focus of intense political debate, a majority of Australians suddenly thought that immigration was too high. Their concerns abated again in 2019. Why? Well, we can't be certain, but it seems likely that it was political discourse that drove public discourse, and not vice versa. The good news, though, is that in three out of the four years we're looking at, most people reported contentment with the level of immigration intake or even wanted more of it. This is an important take-home, and something to celebrate.

FIGURE 4.3 Public opinion on immigration intake,
Australia, by age, 2019[25]

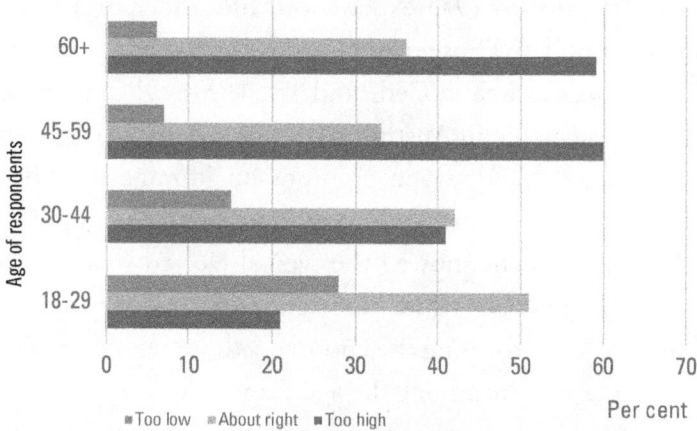

But what lies beneath these aggregate national statistics? Age is one important factor: Australians aged under 45 years report much higher levels of satisfaction with current levels of immigration or desire to increase it than people aged over 45, as Figure 4.3 illustrates.

Most Australian adults aged under 30 reported immigration to be about right. When you add the people in this age group reporting immigration intake to be too low, that means almost 80 per cent show support. Compare this to the response for people aged 45 years and over. What a difference. An outright majority of people aged 45 and over say immigration to Australia is excessive: for those aged between 45 and 59, it's 60 per cent, and for those aged 60 and over it's just a little below that. Why is that, and does it matter? The short answers are history, and yes.

Let's consider those ages again. Anyone living in Australia prior to 1975 experienced life under the White Australia policy. Those over 60 were already adults before the policy was abandoned, and lived through an era of enormous change in Australia. It's not surprising, then, to see the age breakdown in opinions on immigration. But why does that matter? Well, for a start, analysis of the last federal parliament showed the typical elected representative in Australia is a white man aged 51.[26] The very people responsible for running the country – those who draft and pass our laws – are among the age demographic most likely to oppose higher levels of immigration. Further, the Australian electorate is dominated by older people – another result of population ageing. Our politicians are well aware of the predominance of these voters – voters who grew up under the White Australia policy and still have a 'White Australia' mentality, suspicious or fearful of the change that immigrants bring.

What's most interesting, though, is that young people – the ones facing life in a very different workforce and economic climate, and grappling with housing and job insecurity – are happy with the current immigration intake, or think it should be increased. Young people are in direct competition, if you like, with migrants, but instead of fearing them, younger people tend to be more accepting. Perhaps they're aware that migrants help to ease the socioeconomic pressures facing younger people in Australia. An interesting question is whether our perceptions of and attitudes towards migrants change as we age, but it's one not easily answered. Only time and data will tell.

The way we respond to change as we age is another likely factor contributing to the split between older and younger Australians. As a nation, we've undergone a massive transition from a predominantly white country with a British heritage to a multicultural society made up of people from countries all around the world. But to understand how Australians view this change, we need to unpack the data. The Lowy poll fortunately included a number of other questions that allow us to examine this issue in more depth. Figure 4.4 sets out respondents' answers, breaking them down by age group.

On whether Australian cities are overcrowded due to immigration, overall Australians say yes. There is an age gradient here, with people aged over 45 years reporting substantially higher levels of agreement. This question is a tricky one. While migrants have contributed to population growth, in the longer term it's been babies bumping the population along – but as we've discussed already, perceptions are sometimes more powerful than reality. People who spend hours every day sitting in traffic or crushed in public transport feel they're competing for resources, and it's not unusual to hear this blamed on migrants. It's not migrants' fault, though, that people all want to be at work by 9 and knock off around 5 – outdated infrastructure and inefficient modes of work and travel are to blame.

Australians of all ages agree that, overall, migrants have a positive impact on the economy. Again, an age

FIGURE 4.4 Public opinion on immigration matters, Australia, 2019[27]

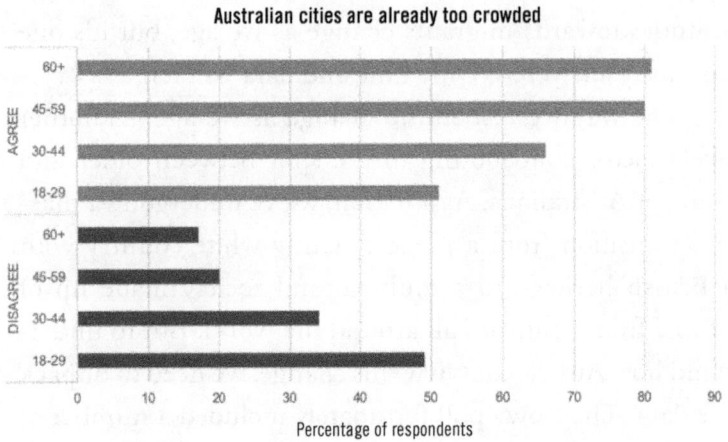

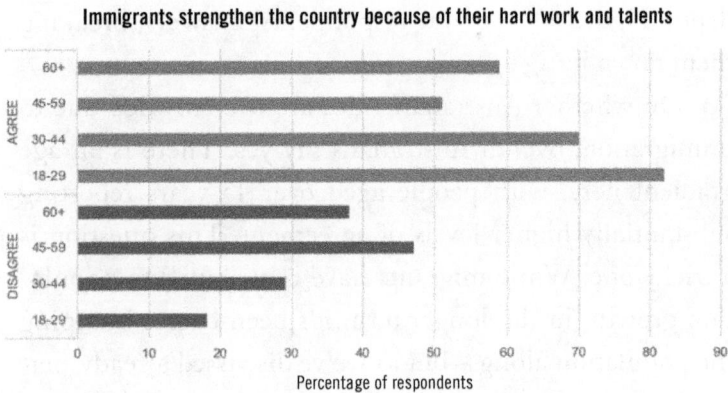

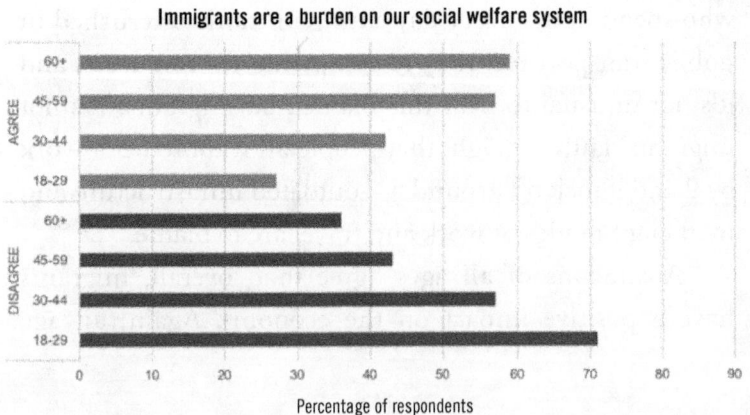

Overall, immigration has a positive impact on the economy of Australia

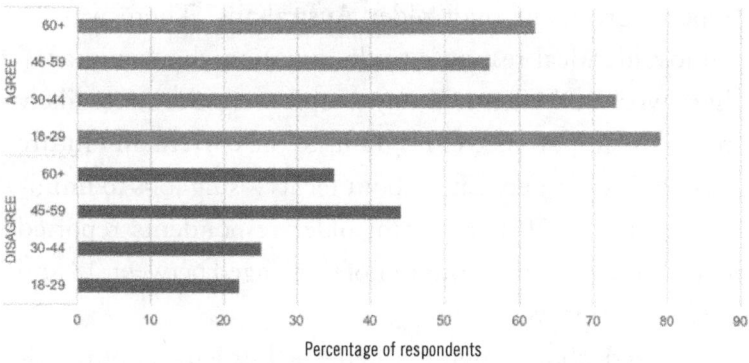

Immigrants take away jobs from other Australians

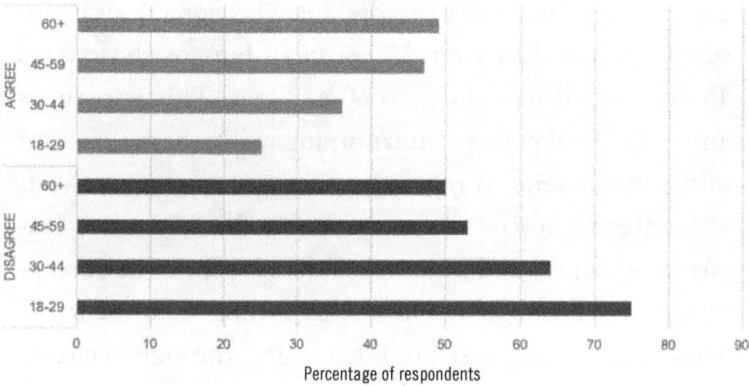

Accepting immigrants from many different countries makes Australia stronger

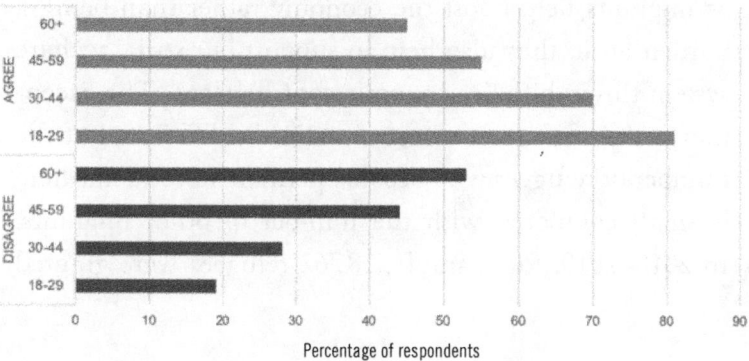

gradient is evident: younger people are more likely to report agreement than older Australians. There was an almost identical response to the question about migrants' hard work and talents. Young people were also more likely to see the importance of migrants to the current and future labour force: when asked about locals losing jobs to immigrants, nearly 50 per cent of older respondents reported concern, while only a quarter of those aged between 18 and 29 shared this worry.

Asked about migrants being a burden on our welfare system, older people again reported greater levels of concern: the number of under-30s who agreed with this statement was just over 25 per cent, but for those aged 45 and over it was closer to 60 per cent. This is perhaps another case of perception trumping reality. Some sections of the media tend to represent migrants as welfare cheats who take advantage of the system at the Australian taxpayers' expense, and older Australians seem to be susceptible to this message. It couldn't be further from the truth. Migrants pay their way (and then some, through taxation) and, as I mentioned earlier, they cannot use the Australian welfare system, including Medicare, for support. Just as migrants help boost the economy rather than being a burden on it, they also help to support our social welfare system through their economic contributions. The exception here is refugees, whose situation is different, but the number of refugees who become permanent residents here is small compared with the number of other migrants. In 2018–2019, for example, 18 762 refugees were granted permanent residence in Australia, versus 160 323 people accepted through the migration program.[28] This is in any case a separate question, and should be treated as such: it is Australia's duty as a global citizen to have a strong refugee program.

There are further questions here begging to be asked. Do older people fear change while younger people see possibilities? Are older people more likely to accept what they see or hear in the media than younger people? For me, the answers to these questions can also be found in the data generated by the Lowy poll. The attitudes of the different age groups towards Australia accepting migrants from many different countries might just be the key to what's going on here.

The starkest difference between the age groups is in their response to the idea that difference brings strength. More than half of the respondents aged 60 or over – those with the most direct exposure to the White Australia policy – did not agree that there is strength in the diversity that migrants bring to our society, whereas a majority of those under 60 supported this statement. My take is that these age differences in attitudes towards immigration indicate fear of the other, fear about what locals stand to lose. Our politicians actively capitalise on these fears, despite knowing they're unfounded, because they know it will win them votes. As workers and as taxpayers, migrants help to build Australian homes, hospitals, schools and roads. They help to staff hospitals, aged-care facilities, child-care centres, places of education and public transport systems. The populist tactic of questioning migrants' contributions does damage to us all.

All rise, Boomer

Since they first starting voting, the baby boomers have represented a large and potentially powerful bloc. Their generation was the first in the 20th century to grow up in a time of peace (albeit an uncertain peace), and the first to witness such sustained economic growth, giving them a confidence and optimism their parents' generation hadn't known. They were the generation who voted for Whitlam, helping to bring about an end to the White Australia policy, and they were the first to mount a significant attack on the gender barriers faced by Australian women. The oldest boomers have been retired for some time now, while the youngest are approaching their mid-50s and looking forward to retirement, but they continue to play an active role in Australia's political, social and cultural life.

Australian Electoral Commission data, used to compile the electoral roll for federal elections, shows a roughly equal distribution across the ages 20 to 69 and a clear jump in enrolled people aged 70 and over. Unfortunately, the voting data is aggregated in age groups, and the final category, '70 plus', is extremely broad. What the data shows, though, is that nearly half of all voters enrolled in Australia (48 per cent) are aged 50 years or over. In other words, baby boomers comprise a big chunk of all voters (along with their parents and older siblings, born before the baby boom, and a few of the older members of 'generation X', born in the late 1960s). Not all people belonging to a particular age group will vote in a particular way, of course, but their shared lived and historical experiences mean that they have a lot in common. For politicians, the temptation is too great to resist: baby boomers can be offered incentives, designed specifically for them, to encourage them to vote in a certain way. Why is this a problem? Because the money these politicians have to play with is a pie: it's finite. Give something to one group, and others pay the price. The 2019 federal election was a prime example of how homing in on one section of the population to win votes can lead to some unexpected outcomes.

The Labor opposition campaigned on a platform of reform and was favoured to win the election, based on polling. A lot of polling. The Liberal government opposed Labor's proposed reforms, championing the status quo. Soon it was all about Labor's proposed changes to the franking credit system and negative gearing – tax breaks enjoyed chiefly by wealthier Australians. Population did get a mention, but the election was largely fought on whether older people, especially self-funded retirees, would lose out under the Labor reforms.

The government seized on the controversy over franking credits, organising a series of 'town hall' meetings, which garnered much media attention. The rooms often filled with mostly silver-haired men in boat shoes.[29] The proceedings were likened to a 'very nerdy gameshow', with

FIGURE 4.5 Enrolled electors, Australia, by age group,
30 June 2019[30]

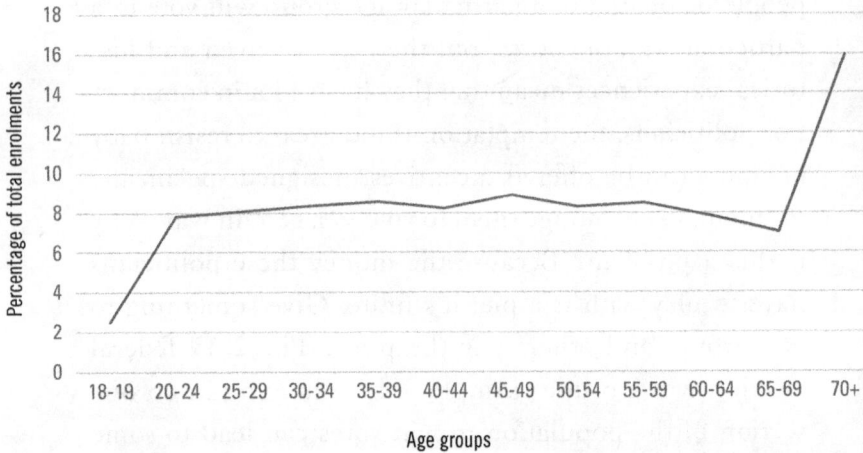

audiences applauding speakers who showed support for the franking credit system and heckling anyone who dared suggest that it be abolished.[31] The Liberal party painted themselves as champions of hard-done-by Australians being kicked in the guts by Labor in their retirement years after working and saving hard their entire lives. It was spin, but it worked. Indignant baby boomers voted for the Liberals, fearing the loss of their retirement income, and Labor lost what had widely been considered an 'unlosable' election.

Getting rid of negative gearing was another major policy element in the Labor arsenal. The original aim of negative gearing, introduced in 1922, was to keep rents affordable by making more housing available, but it wasn't

widely used until the 1980s.[32] The unintended consequence of negative gearing, as I mentioned in the previous chapter, has been to make it easier for investors to buy
property and harder for first homeowners. This perverse
policy favours ... older Australians. Yet again. See where
I'm going with this? Age and retirement became political
dynamite. And, by gosh, it was used well. The handiwork
of the Liberal government was masterful. Retirees – even
those without investment properties or share portfolios
who were living on the age pension – believed they would
suffer under the reforms proposed by Labor. The Labor
party did a terrible job of explaining the proposed changes,
using terminology that bamboozled even the smartest of
people.

Missing from the debate were the real issues facing
Australian baby boomers. One of these issues was what
demographers call the 'feminisation of ageing'. Women
live longer than men, as you may remember from Chapter 2, yet women typically haven't amassed enough superannuation by the time they retire to live well in their old
age. Homelessness is growing among older Australians,
particularly for older women.[33] Add to this the pressure
placed on women to provide unpaid care for grandchildren, potentially while caring for older family members at
the same, sandwiched between the competing demands of
different generations while trying to look after themselves
as well. Such responsibilities reduce the opportunity to
do paid work, too. The economic benefits that accrue to a
family when grandparents look after their grandchildren

flow more often to the children's parents than the grand-parents, as the parents don't have to pay for care. This also adds to the inequalities we inherit from our parents, as discussed in the last chapter – the haves are doing really well for themselves not having to pay for child care, while the have-nots are feeling the strain of having to stretch their incomes further to cover the costs of child care.

If you're still not convinced of the real nature of the social and economic pressures faced by older Australians, and particularly older women, think about those people who've been dubbed 'elder orphans'. Falling family sizes and an increasing number of singles in Australian society have contributed to a lack of familial support for older people. In other words, those with smaller families or no children at all may have no one to help care for them or provide social support in their older years. The rights of people living in aged care have become a major issue in Australia in recent years, as the boomer cohort ages. There have been numerous scandals involving the abuse of older Australians living in nursing homes: residents not being fed nutritious meals, for example, and in the very worst cases being neglected, physically mistreated or even subjected to violence. Financial abuse of elderly people has become another prominent issue, which perhaps has something to do with growing generational inequality: children wanting to get their hands on what they think of as 'their' money before their parents can spend it. Quality health care, full and ongoing social participation and a feeling of personal safety and financial security are all fundamental to successful ageing. Australia hasn't done well so far in providing these things to older people, nor in supporting them to continue to live autonomously in their homes for as long as possible.

There's massive political advantage in selling your message to baby boomers, yet they're being sold a dud. Unscrupulous politicians seeking votes have persuaded them to see problems where there are none – and all the while the real issues confronting older Australians are overlooked and neglected. A cynic might go so far as to say that politicians are really only motivated by their own needs, not those of the nation.

*

When it comes to population, it's not growth we should be panicking about. Some aspects of Australia's demography are definitely cause for alarm, but overcrowding is the least of our worries. Problematising population makes a problem of us – but we're not the problem. Social division, growing inequality, generational tug-of-war, pressures on women to have children, and the lack of a coherent plan for the future in the form of a population policy – these are the issues we should be screaming about, stomping our feet and demanding action. These are the issues that threaten us now, and in the future. But what can we do to fix them? That's what we'll look at in Part III: 'The future of us'.

PART III

The future of us

CHAPTER 5

Demographic prospects

We're standing here, on the precipice of the future. What possibilities await? What decisions need to be made? How fast do we need to act? To find out the answers, we need to ask even more questions: What and who do we want to be as a nation? What values are important to us as a society? What are we willing to do to make change? And how do we get people on board? We know how we got here, and the problems we're dealing with. But what are the possible solutions?

We're facing change like we've never seen before – change that will go beyond social norms, perhaps even beyond demography. Our aim must be to hand the nation over to the next generation confidently, knowing that we've been responsible – that we haven't made a mess and left them to clean it up, or even robbed them of their future altogether. But what is it that Australia needs to plan for? What demographic pressures will we face in the future?

Get ready. There's more data coming your way.

Projecting possibilities

Efforts to project future population can be fraught with uncertainty. In fact, the approach demographers typically use actually prevents the calculation of odds. First we make assumptions – about births, deaths and migration, and where the numbers are headed – and then we use these assumptions to make projections. We base these initial assumptions on past events – but the past may not always be a good indication of where the future is headed. Sometimes things just happen that can't be anticipated or explained. In other words, we have no way to determine how likely it is that our assumptions will prove correct. At the end of the day, though, we need to base our plans on something – so we go with the methods we have, despite their uncertainty.

The data we use for this purpose in Australia comes mainly from the Australian Bureau of Statistics. Every five years, after the national census, the ABS publishes population projections looking 50 years into the future. Projections looking any further ahead than that tend to be very shaky – in fact, things start to wobble after only about ten years, and get more and more wobbly the further into the future we go, as we head away from the known and deeper and deeper into the unknown.

The strength of the Australian Bureau of Statistics projections is that the assumptions they make about fertility, mortality and migration are made in consultation with a range of experts outside the bureau. They set expected fertility rates, life expectancy and migration levels in accordance with past trends, while taking into consideration potential changes in underlying demographic factors, government policy and social behaviours. The reason that the ABS projections are so valuable to people like me is that they are calculated and published at arm's length from the federal government, unlike, say, the estimates and projections produced by Treasury.

The bureau publishes high-, medium- and low-range projections, referred to as series A, B and C, respectively. From a demographer's point of view – in fact from almost anyone's point of view – it is the medium-range series B projections that are the most useful, as they avoid the extremes represented by series A and C. The most recent projections, looking from 2018 ahead to 2066, assume a high fertility rate of 1.95 births per woman, a medium rate of 1.8 births, and a low rate of 1.65 births. (I'm simplifying things here slightly to make all this easier to follow, leaving out the details about how assumptions are phased in over time.) In the following discussion, I'll be using the mid-range figure of 1.8 births per woman, which reflects the actual fertility rate observed for women in Australia between 2014 and 2016. I'll also be using the mid-range figures for life expectancy: 83 years for men, and 86 for women.[1]

Why do we need these projected figures, though? Well, once we've decided to accept the mid-range figures for fertility and mortality, we can start exploring the effects migration might have on Australian society over the next 50 years. What we're doing, essentially, is making fertility and mortality our constants, assuming they'll remain unchanged while we tweak migration levels. This allows us to isolate net overseas migration as the only variable, so we can test different assumptions about future levels of immigration and make projections about the impact it will have.

Net overseas migration to Australia for 2018 was 248 400, with a four-year average of 230 200 annually between 2015 and 2018. The ABS projections are based on assumptions ranging from a low of 175 000 people each year to a high of 275 000, with the mid-range projection sitting exactly halfway between, at 225 000. Assuming that fertility and mortality remain in the mid-range, it is clear that Australia's population is set to increase whether immigration intake is high, medium, low or zero, as Figure 5.1 shows. The only difference between these four scenarios is that population would eventually begin to decline if the intake were zero. The decline would start in 2040, with total population dropping by fewer than 3000 people in that year. It would then fall further each year, with a drop of nearly 90 000 people in 2066.

A decline in the population doesn't necessarily mean problems. It's not how much you have but what you do with what you've got that matters, after all. It's still a risk, though, and an extreme one. A risk that demographers, economists and high-profile businesspeople, among others, have been warning of for quite some time now.[2] The biggest problem is that a declining Australian population without migration to bolster it would be older and

FIGURE 5.1 Population projections in varying migration scenarios, Australia, 2017–2066[3]

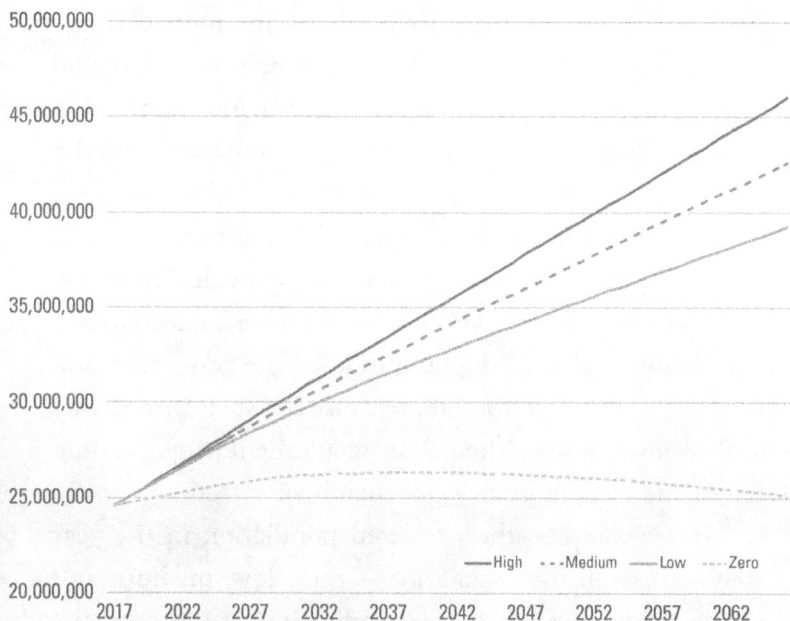

Note: Medium-range assumptions are used for fertility and life expectancy, consistent with ABS series B projections.

more unequal than it is today. An older population could also compound the low fertility rates we already see, pushing them down even further – well below the replacement rate – to around one birth per woman. It's near impossible to breathe life back into fertility rates once they fall so low.

Yi Fuxian, a Chinese demographer, has called population decline a 'humanitarian catastrophe' and argues, convincingly, that its catastrophic effects have a special impact on women.[4] With a declining population, the pressure on us increases – to have children, and more of them, to care for the elderly, to participate in paid work too, and to keep doing all the household stuff at the same time. Ooooff, I'm shattered just writing that sentence. I need a lie-down.

The good news, of course, is that Australia would never cut immigration altogether – we're too dependent on it – so at the national level, at least, we have no need to fear population decline. I'm going to keep the zero-migration scenario in the mix, though, because it's such a good way to demonstrate what the results would be if people calling for an end to immigration got their way.

If we compare the projected population in the year 2040 across all four scenarios – zero, low, medium and high intake – we get a good indication of the potential futures we're facing. (As noted, 2040 is the year in which the first decline occurs in the zero-migration scenario.) The total population in the zero-migration scenario is projected to be 26.3 million. Not much of an increase on today's population. This is compared with 32.4 million in the low-migration scenario, 33.6 million in the medium-migration scenario, and 34.8 million in the high-migration scenario. It's important to note, however, that this says nothing about the composition of the population – which is what really matters. Australia could have a population of just over 26 million people, but if they were mostly over 70, we'd be in trouble. After all, it's the working-age population who hold up the economy.

The message here is: Beware focusing on the quantum. Size isn't everything. In fact, size is almost meaningless. People calling for cuts to immigration often make this mistake. They are happy to advocate for a population of a certain size – but whatever that population's size might be, they rarely seem to think about its age composition. They fail to recognise that it's not the number of people Australia needs to focus on but rather the population's economic sustainability – and, as we've already seen, an economically sustainable population is one that has a good chunk of people of working age.

So what would happen to the age composition of the Australian population under the various migration scenarios? I'm glad you asked. Let's look all the way ahead to 2066. The result of the zero-migration scenario after 50 years would be a population of 25.1 million, while the low-, medium- and high-migration scenarios would see projected populations of 39.2 million, 42.6 million and 46 million people, but what we're interested in is the age structure of these populations. Figure 5.2 shows how the zero-, low-, medium- and high-migration scenarios would translate into population composition.

What's most concerning about the zero-migration scenario is that the largest group of women are 85 and over. This is the feminisation of ageing we've talked about. Imagine the humanitarian catastrophe that might result from a steadily ageing female population within a couple of generations. Inadequate pensions, insufficient

FIGURE 5.2 Population age and sex structure in varying migration scenarios, Australia, 2066[5]

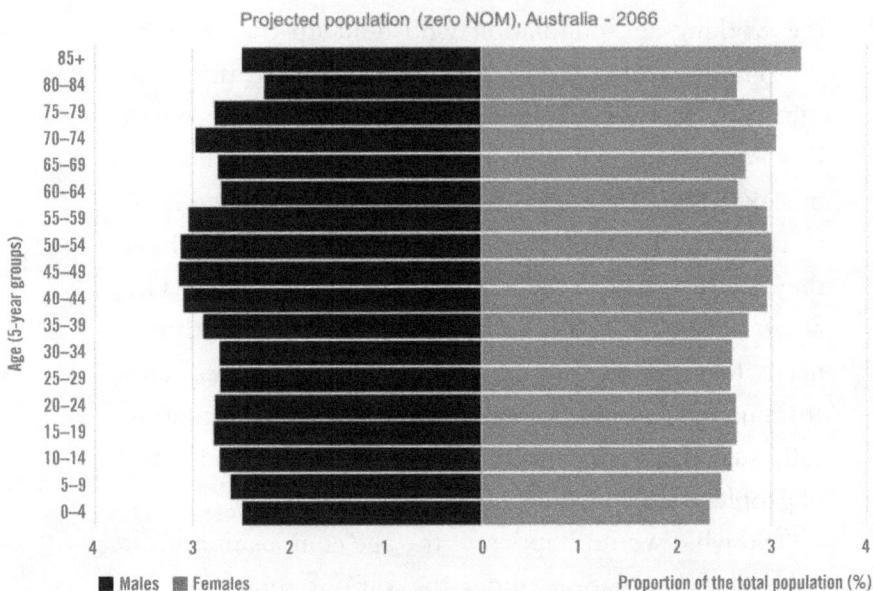

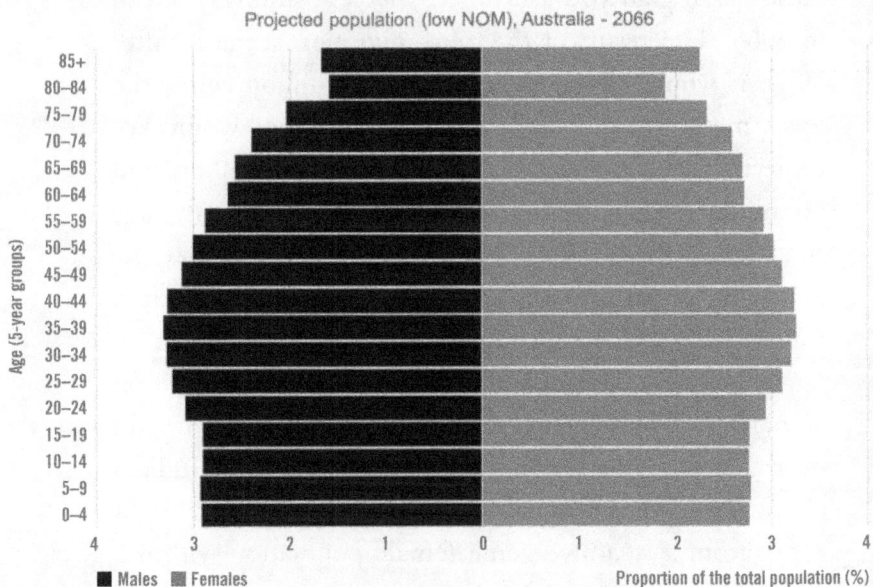

Projected population (zero NOM), Australia - 2066

Projected population (low NOM), Australia - 2066

Demographic prospects

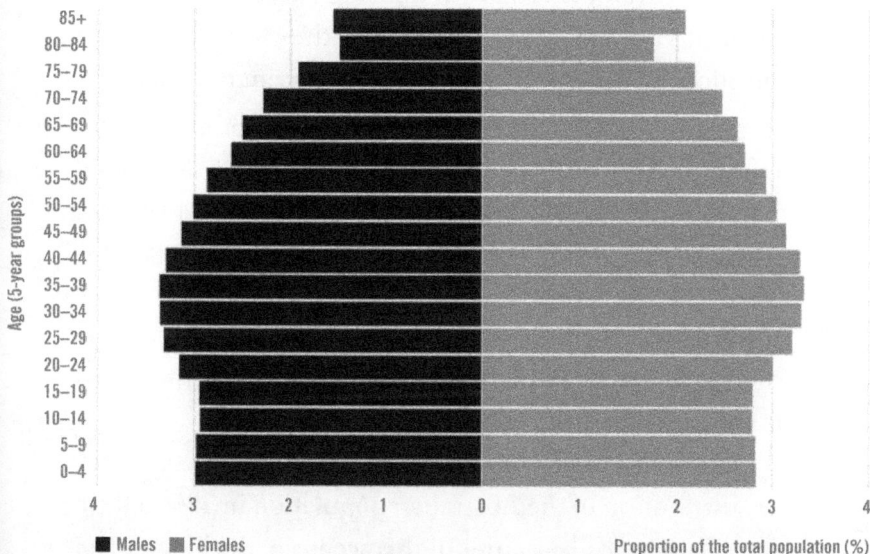

Projected population (medium NOM), Australia - 2066

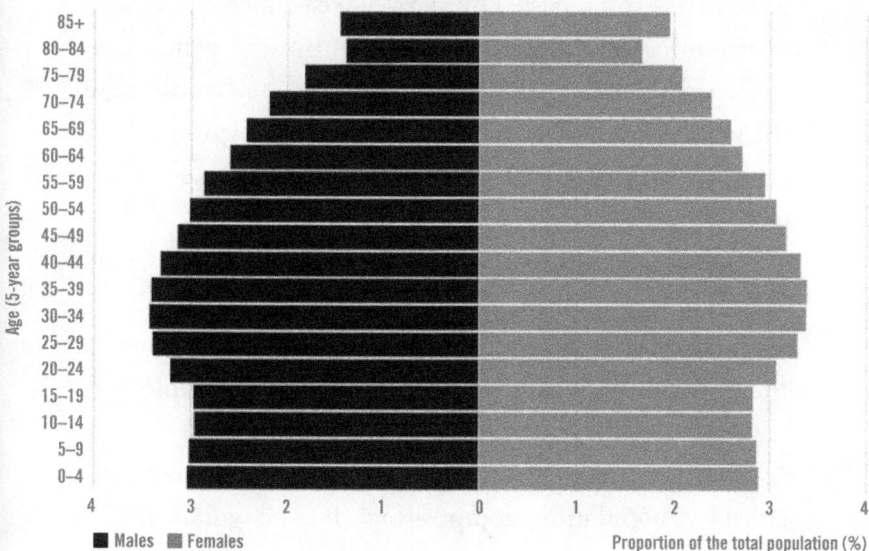

Projected population (high NOM), Australia - 2066

NOTE NOM stands for 'net overseas migration'.

superannuation, shortfalls in housing and a growing need for aged care are just a few of the things we'd need to consider. In this same zero-migration scenario, the largest group of men would be those aged between 45 and 49 years. That might sound slightly more encouraging – after all, these are men of working-age – but just look where the bulk of the population is concentrated. Yep, right across the ages leading up to retirement. We'd definitely have to kiss retirement goodbye in this scenario, because there aren't enough people coming up through the ranks to replace retirees leaving the workforce.

Low net overseas migration would make the age and sex distribution of the Australian population in 2066 a little more economically secure. In this scenario, the biggest age group for both women and men is that between 35 and 39. There's still a large chunk of older women (and a not-quite-so-large chunk of older men), but the genders are more evenly balanced in older age than they would be in the zero-migration scenario. The number of young people looks promising, and the bulk of the population sits closer to the middle of the working-age range.

In the medium- and high-migration scenarios, both the total population and the working-age population are younger again. So too is the largest age group within the population, with the greatest number of people aged between 30 and 39.

It's very clear. Any talk about population size must consider population composition. It's no good striving for a size or particular growth rate if the balance of older and younger people is so badly out that it puts the nation's future in danger. Migrants not only provide the Australian workforce with much needed labour and skills, but they also help to shore up future generations. While migrants come to Australia already part way through life, they are on average younger and, as noted previously, contribute to future Australian generations by having children and raising them here.

We've talked about the need for enough people of working age to support the total population. But how exactly does that relate to the number of jobs? In 2017, it was estimated that by 2024, more than 4 million new jobs would be created in Australia.[6] That's a need for more than 4 million new people in the workforce. There's no way that we can fill all those new jobs without migration.

But it's not just new jobs needing to be filled. Every time someone leaves a job, they need to be replaced. Demand for replacement workers is generally highest in jobs with greater turnover, but at present it's chiefly due to the retirement of baby boomers. With people ageing out of the workforce, a great deal of experience will be lost. If the past is anything to go by – and we know it is – the demand for employees can only be met by net overseas migration. The local population simply can't replace those leaving the workforce, largely because of the sheer number of those leaving, but also due to skill shortages and a lack of people able and willing to enter particular job markets.

We've looked at population prospects at the national level now, but there's more to this question. We all live in

Australia, yes, but our everyday lives have a much smaller circumference. What might our states, territories and major cities look like, population-wise, in the future? Using the same projection methods and the same four migration scenarios again, let's consider New South Wales, Victoria and Queensland and their capital cities first – the three main destinations for migrants – and then take a look at other parts of Australia. Figure 5.3 shows us that, just like the national population, the New South Wales and Sydney populations would increase, at least initially, under any net migration scenario: zero, low, medium or high. The same applies to Victoria and its capital city, Melbourne, as Figure 5.4 illustrates, and Queensland and its capital city, Brisbane, as Figure 5.5 illustrates.

The zero-migration scenario would lead to a decline in population for Sydney and New South Wales beginning in 2032. In New South Wales, the drop in that first year would be around 1700 people; by 2066, the annual drop would reach 44 000. Sydney would experience a greater decline, with a drop of just over 2000 people in 2032, ending with an annual drop of 32 600 people come 2066. This thought might please some, especially as the population of New South Wales would reach 7.2 million and Sydney's would reach 4.7 million by 2066, despite the projected decline. But remember, it's not the number of people that's important; it's the composition of the population. And we know, having looked at the national scenario, that things could go horribly wrong without the youthful injection that migration brings.

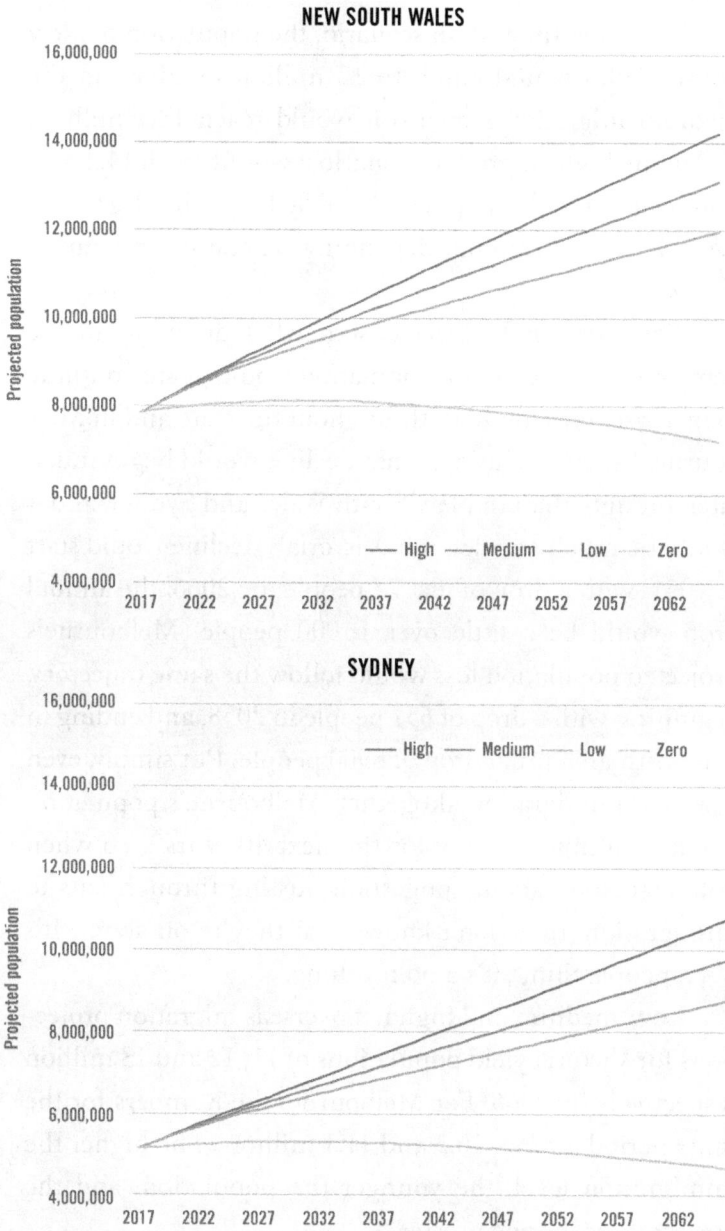

FIGURE 5.3 Population projections in varying migration scenarios, New South Wales (above) versus Sydney (below), 2017–2066[7]

NOTE Medium-range assumptions are used for fertility, life expectancy and net internal migration, consistent with ABS series B projections.

In the low-migration scenario, the population of New South Wales would climb to 12 million by 2066; in the medium-migration scenario it would reach 13.1 million, and in the high-migration scenario it would reach 14.2 million. Similarly, the population of Sydney would grow to 8.8, 9.7 or 10.7 million, depending on the net migration intake.

The story in Victoria is somewhat different. In the zero-migration scenario, population would again continue to increase, initially, both throughout the state and in Melbourne, before declining. That decline would begin much later, though, than in New South Wales and Sydney, and it would be much smaller, too. Victoria's decline would start in 2051, with a drop of just 77 people; by 2066, the annual drop would be a little over 16000 people. Melbourne's projected population loss would follow the same trajectory, beginning with a drop of 651 people in 2058, and ending in 2066 with an annual drop of 8900 people. Put simply, even if we cut immigration altogether, Melbourne's population would continue to grow for the next 40 years – so when politicians talk about congestion-busting through cuts to immigration, they don't know what they're on about. It's not a people thing, it's a policy thing.

Low, medium and high net overseas migration projections for Victoria yield populations of 11, 12 and 13 million respectively by 2066. For Melbourne, the numbers for the same period are 9.3, 10.2 and 11.1 million. The higher the immigration level, the younger the population, and the greater its economic prospects.

FIGURE 5.4 Population projections in varying migration scenarios, Victoria (above) versus Melbourne (below), 2017–2066[8]

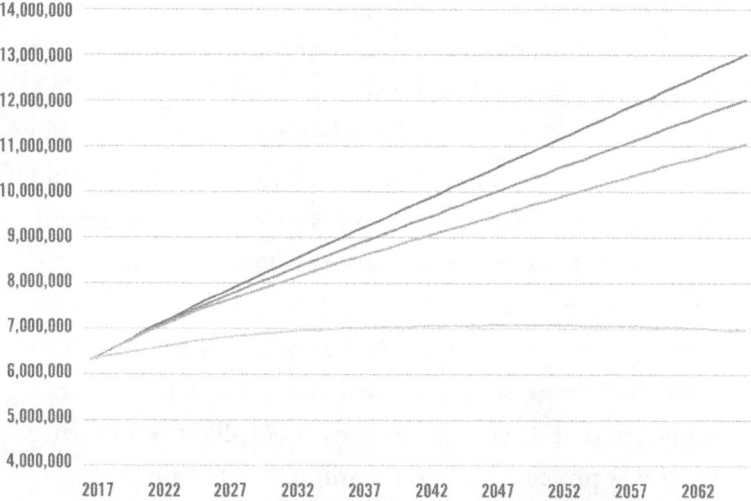

VICTORIA

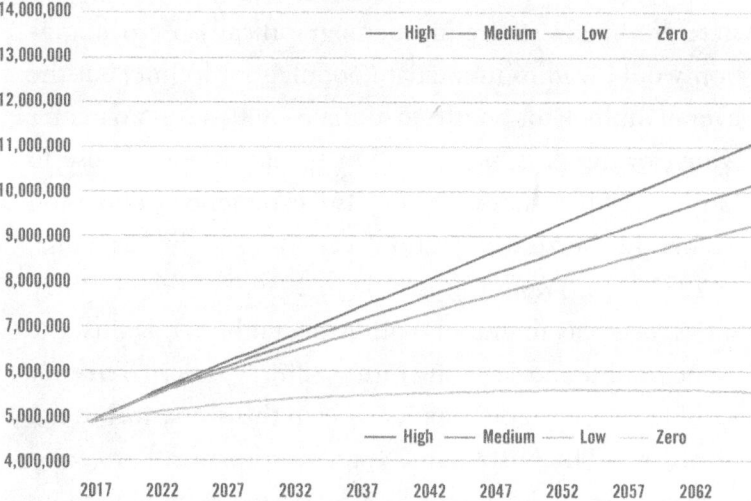

MELBOURNE

NOTE Medium-range assumptions are used for fertility, life expectancy and net internal migration, consistent with ABS series B projections.

Queensland is the third most populous state in Australia, with Brisbane and the surrounding coastal cities home to the third highest number of recent migrants. The projections here reveal a fascinating story. Even in the zero-migration scenario, the population of Queensland only starts to decline a few years before our 50-year cut-off. It's projected to drop by 247 people in 2061, with the annual decline to hit a little over 3100 by 2066, which would make the state's total population in that year 5.8 million. And there's no decline projected for Brisbane at all. The city's population will still be going up in 2066, albeit at a slowing rate, and is projected to hit 3.1 million that same year.

Projections for the remaining states and territories are presented in Figure 5.6. The case of South Australia is the stand-out. With the oldest population of all, the state is already struggling demographically. Zero migration would lead to immediate population decline, but the overall outlook for South Australia is pretty grim no matter which of the possible migration scenarios you choose to look at. Other states would also experience population decline in the zero-migration scenario: first in Tasmania, in 2027, then Western Australia in 2046. For both of these states, overseas migration will be a vital buffer against the demographic shocks of the future. The Northern Territory would also face population decline in this scenario, but not until 2065. The Australian Capital Territory isn't projected to decline at all during the 50-year period, with or without overseas immigration.

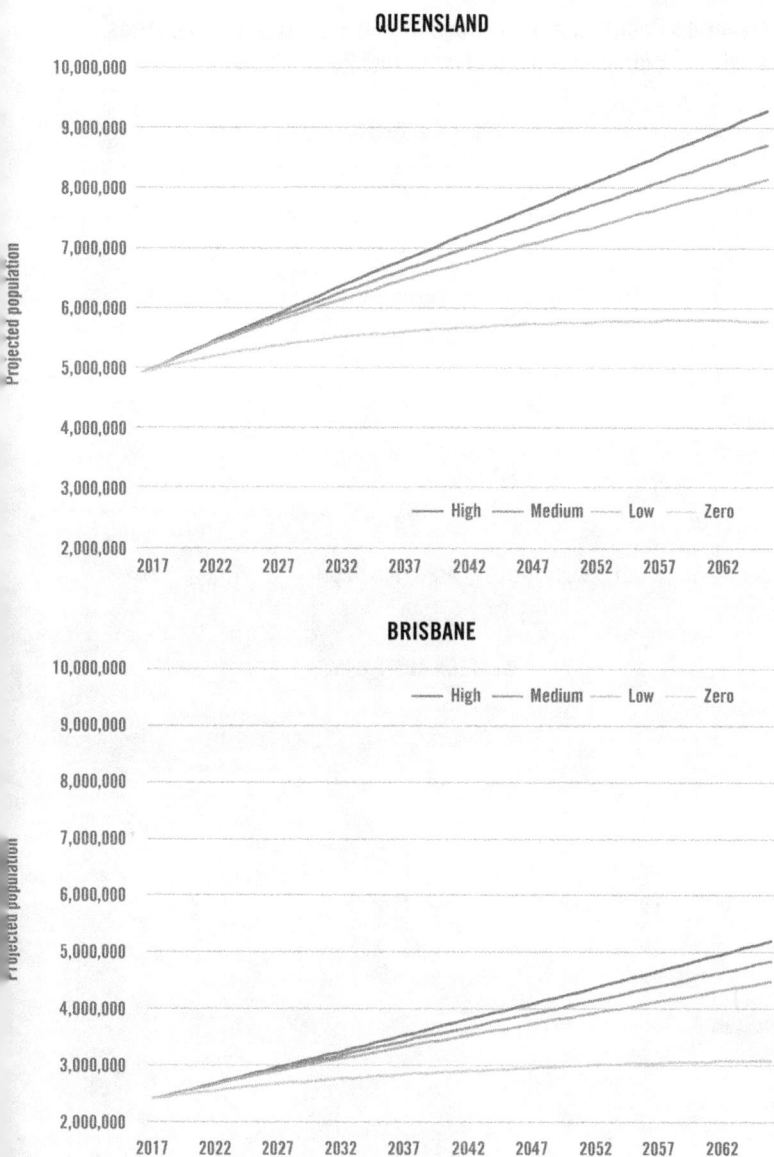

FIGURE 5.5 Population projections in varying migration scenarios, Queensland (above) versus Brisbane (below), 2017–2066[9]

NOTE Medium-range assumptions are used for fertility, life expectancy and net internal migration, consistent with ABS series B projections.

FIGURE 5.6 Population projections in varying migration scenarios, other states and territories, 2017–2066[10]

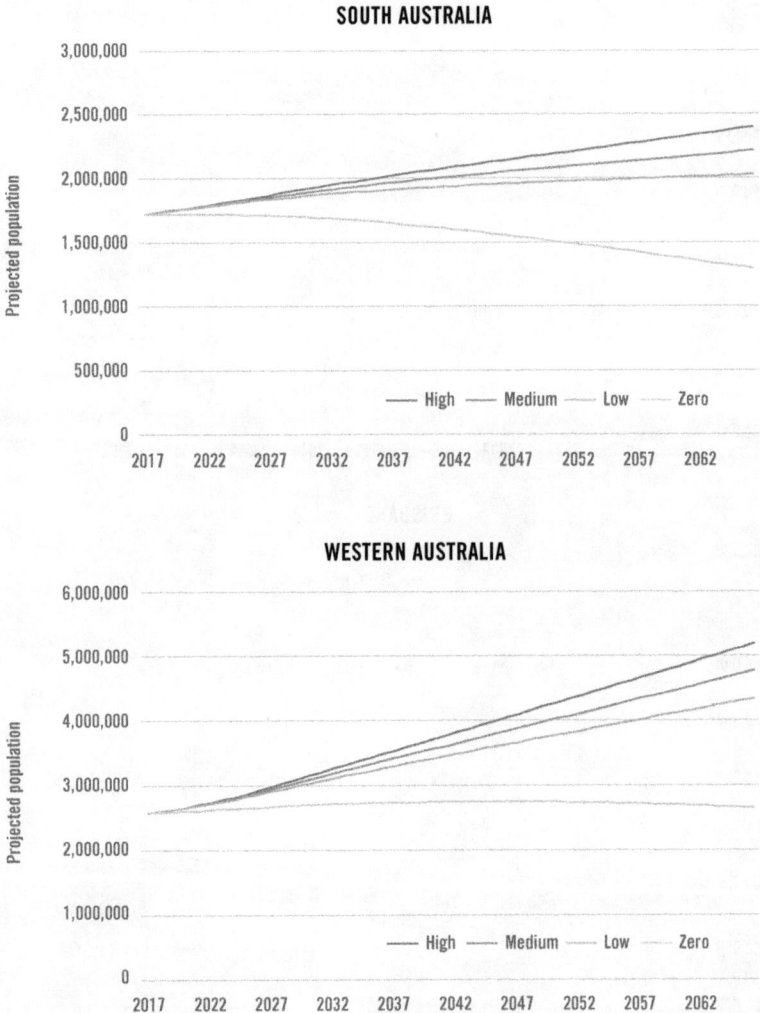

SOUTH AUSTRALIA

WESTERN AUSTRALIA

NOTE Medium-range assumptions are used for fertility, life expectancy and net internal migration, consistent with ABS series B projections.

TASMANIA

Projected population

Year	
2017	

— High — Medium — Low — Zero

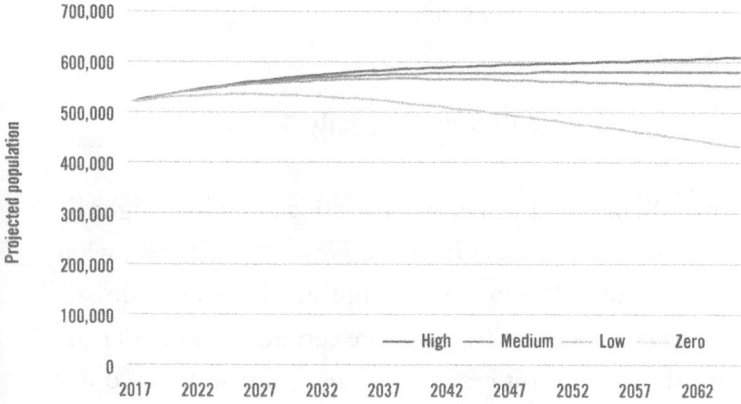

NORTHERN TERRITORY

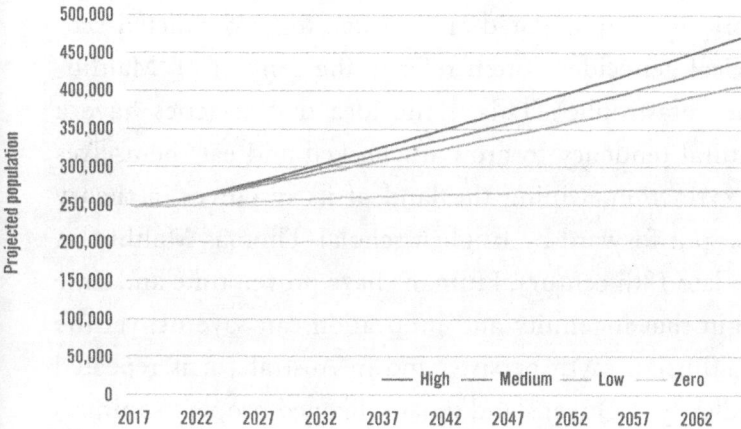

Projected population

— High — Medium — Low — Zero

AUSTRALIAN CAPITAL TERRITORY

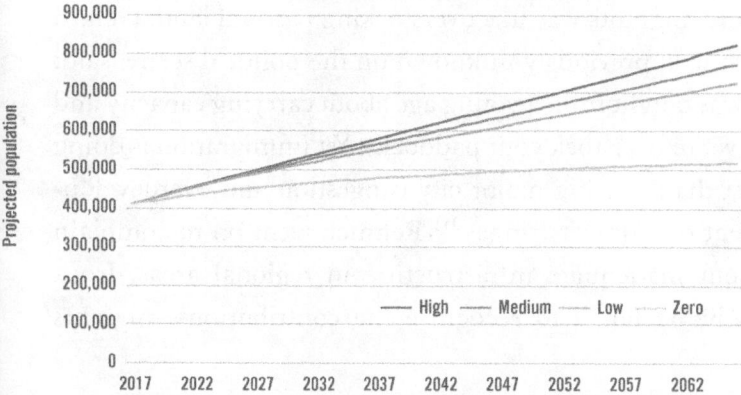

Projected population

— High — Medium — Low — Zero

Carrying capacity

At any talk of possibilities, or projections of what might lie ahead, uncertainty rears its head. None of us knows what the future holds. We can take an optimistic or a pessimistic view, but neither gives us any more certainty – so under the circumstances, isn't it better to be an optimist, focused not on problems but potential solutions?

Population pessimists – those with the view that the world is overpopulated and headed for self-inflicted ecological genocide – often refer to the concept of 'Malthusian catastrophe'. This is the idea that societies have a natural tendency to grow unchecked and eat themselves to extinction, wiping the land of its resources, a theory first put forward by English scholar Thomas Malthus in the late 18th century. Humans have proven time and time again that ingenuity and innovation can save us, yet the Malthusian myth persists, and in Australia it is repeated endlessly. A Queensland senator likened people to animals in his maiden speech in 2019, saying that his expertise as a farmer's son led him to believe that Australia taking in more migrants was like overstocking pastoral land. Gerard Rennick, previously unknown on the political scene, said: 'I was taught from a young age about carrying capacity and never to overstock your paddocks. Yet immigration is doing just that, causing major city congestion and overdevelopment on our city fringes.'[11] Rennick went on to complain about inadequate infrastructure in regional areas. Ironically, he failed to recognise the contributions migrants make to building needed infrastructure. But he's not alone, unfortunately.

Rapa Nui (or Easter Island), a small island in Polynesia situated far from any neighbour, has traditionally been held up as the quintessential example of human selfishness and ecological irresponsibility – overstocking of the paddocks, if you will. Demographers have even suggested that what happened there is a real-life example of a Malthusian catastrophe, proving the theory true.[12] The evidence, as reported by geographers and demographers, has centred on the cutting down of trees to facilitate the movement of the large statues for which the island is so well known.[13] The story goes that the land became inhospitable following the removal of the trees, incapable of supporting plant life, and therefore human life. Desperate, the Rapa Nui people turned on each other, first fighting over resources and then resorting to cannibalism, until eventually they became extinct. Powerful story, if only it were true.

Extensive anthropological investigations have come to a very different and much more likely conclusion – one supported by evidence, rather than hypotheses. The islanders of Rapa Nui did not die en masse through their own profligacy; nor was it their land's carrying capacity that drove them close to extinction.[14] Many of them were in fact kidnapped by 19th-century slave-traders from South America. The expeditions of various colonial powers to the island also introduced new species of animals and diseases that ravaged the landscape and its people. By 1877, the population had dwindled so low that only 111 islanders remained. This version of the story might be harder to hear, though. Especially for people living in places with a similar history. Australia being one.

In the absence of certainty, people grasp at straws. It's a normal human response to want to know that the sun will rise each morning after setting the night before, and that the way things have been will always be. This helps explain why, in Australia, calls are made to return to long-term levels of population growth and immigration intake. Mark Latham, once the federal Labor leader and now leader of One Nation in New South Wales, called for the immigration intake to be reduced to the 20th-century average in the lead-up to the 2019 New South Wales state election.[15] At the heart of such approaches to population is the idea that if things return to how they once were, or how they were during the proposer's heyday, then all will be okay. It's like your favourite music. Think about it. The best music is from the 1990s, if you ask me, because it reminds me of when I was young.

Appealing to memories of voters' heydays works particularly well for older cohorts, for people afraid of change, and for people worried that they're not getting a fair go. Promising a return to the past makes these people feel secure: they know the past; they're certain of it. New South Wales Premier Gladys Berejiklian did this effectively during the 2019 state election campaign. The conservative Berejiklian stated that immigration levels should return to the average seen during John Howard's prime ministership, between 1996 and 2007.[16] Evoking Howard's record worked; his popularity, as evidenced by his longevity as prime minister, coupled with his ability to ride the grey vote, gave great resonance to the premier's argument for cuts to immigration. The promised cuts haven't eventuated, of course – Berejiklian was bluffing – and nothing remarkable has happened since the election to suggest that they will.

The fear of uncertainty is no better encapsulated than when projections are reported in the media or discussed by non-demographers. Population projections are often misinterpreted as forecasts, and then used to whip up panic about the population's growth rate, or to call the experts into question, especially when growth exceeds expectations. Outdated projections are commonly quoted to stir up concern: the old 'we're growing faster than predicted' line. The 1998 projections, for example, are often quoted by the anti-immigration chorus, but the funny thing is that between 1998 and the present day, it is births, not immigration, that have increased to unexpected levels – the rate of natural increase, not immigration, has been the real surprise. Even journalists make such errors, despite consulting experts.[17]

In fact, comparing population projections from the two most recent Australian Bureau of Statistics publications (see Table 5.2) shows that worries about the Australian population train careering out of control aren't really founded on evidence. The bureau's assumptions changed between 2012 and 2017, and will likely change again in

TABLE 5.2 Population projections, assumptions and outcomes, Australia, 2012 versus 2017

Series	Total fertility rate	Life expectancy		Net overseas migration	Milestones		
		Males	Females		30 million	35 million	40 million
2012	1.8	85	88	240,000	2029/30	2042/43	2056/57
2017	1.8	83	86	225,000	2030/31	2043/44	2058/59

the future – fertility may go down, and possibly mortality too – but the changes weren't dramatic. The milestones of 30 million, 35 million and 40 million were also pushed out, if only by a year or two.

For demographers, there's nothing of concern in these levels of uncertainty: the figures are only intended as a guide. But convincing the public of that is an entirely different matter. Especially when it's a public increasingly distrustful of experts, a public that relies not on evidence but on anecdote and personal observation. And who can we trust, when even the media, whose role it is to keep the public informed, so frequently get even the basics wrong?

Public trust, expertise and what lies beneath

In this 'post-truth' environment of alternative facts and fake news, evidence seems to have become somewhat irrelevant. In Australia, we've seen it take some pretty extreme beatings. Take climate data, for example. Anyone and everyone seems to have an opinion on what's happening and whether the data can be trusted. I often wonder how many of the people commenting on the veracity of climate data have actually looked at the figures rather than relying on obscure blog posts. Anyone with internet access thinks they're an expert now, and the authority of actual experts is called into question as soon as they say something these 'everyday experts' disagree with. I'm not suggesting people aren't entitled to question authority, or the data, or expert opinion. Question away. Questions keep us all honest. What concerns me is the lack of discrimination between good information and bad information – between sources you can trust and sources you can't. It's hell out there. This has been a slow-burning issue, one we've been dealing with for a while now, but if we don't find a way to address it, it could be our very undoing.

Data is vital to a healthy democracy, and society generally. Without it, we'd lack the information we need to formulate policy and face the challenges in our future. Data also supplies the crucial evidence we need to hold government and others in positions of power to account. And a major source of that data is the national census.

In the lead-up to the 2016 census, Tony Abbott's Liberal government instructed the Australian Bureau of Statistics to consider how it could accommodate further funding cuts. The ABS had already been savaged by earlier cuts, and there was little left to trim.[18] A question mark now hung over the future of the census. It is, after all, a major logistical and financial endeavour, the biggest and most expensive undertaken by the Australian government in peacetime. And why wouldn't it be expensive? Every single person in Australia is contacted in some way and enumerated. The ABS considered its options: replacing the five-yearly national data collection with less frequent collections and/or smaller scale undertakings, including a population survey. Government departments were all asked to comment at that time on the potential consequences of the loss of the census, and how the various other options might affect both their departmental work and the nation. This entire exercise was about finding ways to save on costs, and it all occurred on the down low. The media were not aware, and even within government departments it was all done on a need-to-know basis. Secret business. The first the nation heard about the potential end of the census was in an article in the *Sydney Morning Herald* by journalist Peter Martin, by which time a new chief had finally been appointed to the ABS after it had been chief-less for some time, and the proposed end to the census had been knocked on its head.[19]

At the same time, federal parliament was considering new metadata retention laws. Under the guise of keeping the nation safe from terrorism and other criminal activity, the government introduced draft laws to compel telecommunications operators to retain individuals' metadata for two years.[20] Government intelligence and police agencies would have the power to request this telecommunications data. The new laws were debated as preparations were made for the 2016 census. Preparations for the census are usually fairly uncontroversial, but this time, because data retention was already a topic of interest, there was considerable discussion of privacy and potential breaches of privacy.[21]

Concerns about the census and metadata laws weren't the end of it. Distrust of government was heightened in this period, in the wake of growing global anti-establishment sentiment. The nation seemed primed for an upset, and it arrived right on cue. The newly appointed bureau head announced that personal data, including names, addresses and dates of birth, would now be retained for a longer period, though not 'attached' to the main data. The longer retention wasn't really the problem here; rather that these identifiers would make it possible, via statistical means, to link data from the 2016 census to that from previous censuses and other government data. Metadata retention, personal identifiers, linking of data … yep, this was bound to end in a complete shitstorm.

Misinformation was rife, proliferating in mainstream media and all over social media. There was no undoing it. Then misinformation became disinformation. There were calls for boycotts and sabotage. The then senator and deputy leader of the Greens party, Scott Ludlam, even got in on the action, sowing serious seeds of doubt about the capacity of the Australian Bureau of Statistics to keep Australians' data safe and protect it from government misuse.[22] He wasn't the only one. A coalition of politicians from a range of parties urged the public to protest by giving false responses or refusing to fill in the census form. The poor nerds at the ABS. They didn't know what had hit them.

Come the August census night, after all the campaigning and rigmarole in the lead-up to the big moment, the servers supporting the Australian Bureau of Statistics website were taken down by a denial-of-service (DoS) attack. At first it seemed like a case of 'turn it off and back on again', but that didn't work. The vendor tasked with providing the website was found to have insufficiently prepared for the event. The #censusfail hashtag was born. And with that the community pretty much lost faith in the Australian Bureau of Statistics. That faith was somewhat restored following the successful conduct of the Australian marriage law postal survey that paved the way for the legalisation of same-sex marriage – but the #censusfail tag endures.

The census, and data collection in general, became politicised in a way Australia had never seen before. Sure, there's a long, long history of protests around the census, but there had never been anything quite like this. And data, any kind of data, especially that collected or analysed by a government body, became problematic overnight – that fateful census night in August 2016. The good news, however, is that the data from the 2016 census appears to have been unaffected by the chaos. It turns out that when it came down to it, Australians were on the side of information. Analysis of the data by an independent panel of researchers and experts suggests that it's comparable in quality to that of previous censuses.[23]

What was so peculiar about these sudden privacy concerns is that Australians give away sensitive information every day. Facebook, Twitter, Instagram, WhatsApp, credit card transactions – the list goes on. We share our biometric information in the form of photographs that we post online to share with friends and anyone else willing to take the time to scroll through and hit the like button. Women even enter information about their monthly periods, cervical mucus and sexual activity into period- and fertility-tracking apps – what could be more sensitive than that? Businesses are capitalising on all this information, sharing users' information – even their most sensitive information – with third parties.[24] Supermarkets' store loyalty cards are one of the best examples of how our data can be exploited: they are used to track individual spending behaviours, keeping a record of the items we purchase, so that marketing campaigns can be tailored to us personally. So much information is gathered via store loyalty cards that the stores can identify changes in household composition: if you move in with or separate from your partner, for example, or become an empty-nester. Or if you fall pregnant. Most store loyalty card datasets can be used to identify a pregnancy before women have even had time to book their first doctor's appointment, let alone told their family and friends about the growing lump of cells in their womb.

Perhaps we're suspicious because the census is mandatory. On census night, everyone in Australia must complete a form or be included on a form. There are very few exceptions. But Facebook and the others we sign up to? We think we're going in with our eyes open. We think we have control. The sheer act of signing up to a social media platform or loyalty program involves some element of informed consent, even if we don't read the terms and conditions. Who has time for that anyway? The census is different. And the fact that the census is conducted by the government presents red flags for many.

We may not have a census for too much longer anyway. The Abbott government wasn't the first to look into abolishing the census, and the idea was certainly nothing new in the global context: New Zealand and the UK had investigated similar cost savings and data efficiencies in the years prior. The way Australia is headed, we may be looking at a population register as an alternative to the census. If you had concerns about the privacy of census data, you should be more concerned about the alternative. A population register is data collection done unto people, behind closed doors, without their knowledge. You won't know what is known about you, or be able to amend the record if it's not accurate. Think e-tax prefill, only you have absolutely no control over the data or the process.

The population register of the Netherlands is the model Australia would most likely follow. Government data on things like tax and social security is kept for every individual and tracked over time, from cradle to grave. The Dutch system seems to operate well and is accepted by the majority of the population without question, but it can't be taken for granted that such systems are always benign. China has probably the most infamous population register in the world. It acts not just as a dynamic and continuous database, tracking people and providing population facts and figures, but is also used to determine where you can live, where you can go to school and where you can work. China's population register has also been used to enforce the one-child policy through taxes and penalties for people with more than one child. This can have serious consequences: children can't go to school if their birth is not registered, but newborn girls often went unregistered in the past because their parents wanted to keep trying for a son. China has relaxed its one-child policy, but the population register serves as a cautionary tale.

I'd hazard a guess that Australia has maybe two more censuses before the traditional census is substantially altered or even replaced. Before we consider such a move, though, we need to give it serious thought. I want to encourage scepticism, but I also want to discourage needless outrage. I want people to be informed, but not swayed by ideological nonsense. Why? Because unnecessary distrust and suspicion are undermining the vital work done by important institutions, and could end up making things worse for us all.

Without decent social data, we will walk blind into the future, and society will be destined to repeat the wrongdoings of the past. An excellent example of the need for robust data is in looking at questions of gender – which is what I'd like to do next.

Women as gatekeepers: Gender and population

When it comes to population, women have long been seen as problems. They are having too many children, not having enough children, delaying children too long, not caring enough for children, caring too much for children. Population growth and size are all down to women. We look at them and not at men, as though women have children all on their own and no one else is involved. Women are seen as the gatekeepers of our sociodemographic future.

To understand how entrenched this notion is, all you need to do is step back and consider that in 1944 – in the middle of World War II – the Australian government held a royal commission into falling birth rates. Yes, an inquiry was held to get to the bottom of why women weren't having children. Bad women. If you recall, there'd already been a royal commission in 1903, which found that women were reluctant to undergo pregnancy and birth, fearing the disruption children bring, and the loss of life's luxuries. The timing of this new inquiry should have been a big giveaway, if you ask me. Remember what happens to fertility rates during wartime and economic depression? But someone was clearly to blame, and the men were away at war – so who else could be responsible?

The pressure put on women to 'do their duty' is no better summed up than in these two sentences:

You men in easy chairs say 'populate or perish'. Well, I have populated and I perish – with no blankets.[25]

These are the profound words of a woman presenting

her view to the 1944 inquiry. They demonstrate perfectly the immense social and economic pressure placed on women: Just make *it work*. *Have them babies*. Her statement was a direct response to the call to populate the nation, to help strengthen the nation's defence capability. What's best (or thought to be best) for the country can clearly have serious adverse consequences for individuals and their families. Especially women.

All the way back in Chapter 2, I told you to ask someone older than you what gives life its meaning. I said that the answer would likely be family. That's true for both women and men – but if you delve deeper, you're likely to discover that the average woman's take on the responsibilities and pressures of having a family are different to the average man's. Even now, women shoulder the majority of household work (the unpaid stuff) and caring (more unpaid stuff), despite spending increasingly more time in paid employment. Put another way, women are the ones keeping the joint running while men take on the more influential and highly paid work. It's not a choice – it's a gender norm. And even when both the female and male partner in a heterosexual relationship work full time in paid jobs, women still do the largest share of the unpaid (and unseen) labour.[26] (But it's bloody incredible what is seen when the work doesn't get done.)

Demography has a woman problem because society has a woman problem. Our questions often reflect gender norms uncritically. Men aren't asked about children and family-size preferences, while women are often overlooked in discussions of work and career. And much demographic analysis, as you'll have noticed by now, is done through a gendered lens. From the calculation of fertility rates to concerns over declining numbers of children, women are the focus of demographers' preoccupations. And why not, I hear you ask. What's wrong with putting women at the centre of our inquiries? Isn't their experience important? Well, yes, but that gendered lens we look through tends to problematise whomever it is that we're peering at so closely. Why do we only ask how many children the average woman has? Why don't we care how many children the average man has? Women give birth to children, yes, but family isn't, nor should it be, the sole realm of women and their burden to carry.

Binary notions of sex, as distinct from gender, have traditionally underpinned much of the demographer's work. Sex is the term we use to indicate the biological equipment individuals have (or don't have), which is relevant in determining which individuals or groups are 'at risk' of certain life events, such as giving birth. The term gender refers, of course, to the way individuals perceive themselves: whether that's female, male or something else. The interplay of sex and gender is too complex a subject for me to take on here; the important thing to note is that sex is important if we want to understand how childbearing affects an individual's role in society and the subsequent tug of war they are likely to experience between family and work.

Women have for a long time been seen as a potential pool of workers who can and should be drawn on to increase labour force participation in Australia. Yet women are pulled between the expectations of motherhood, other forms of care and paid work. Indeed, many find themselves stuck in the middle of a care sandwich: caring for kids, parents, partners or other loved ones while trying to survive financially. Women are vital to Australia's future. But something has to give … and, no, it's not women that need to give. They're already giving enough. Policy and practice have to get with the times.

*

Population, and demography more specifically, aren't just outcomes to be observed, but rather influential forces that can be harnessed to change a society's course. Demography shapes future possibilities, and it's needed now more than ever to help guide the nation towards the best possible future for us all. Change is necessary: that much is clear. Australia needs to get past its white nationalist shackles and its woman problem and move on. But how can we address these issues? Who should we be listening to? And what do we do next? In the final chapter of this book, I'm going to give you my thoughts on these questions – and set out my own ten-point plan for the coming decades.

CHAPTER 6

Creating opportunities from challenges

The present preoccupation – obsession, really – with population size and growth fails to address the real and immediate problems Australia faces. A potential demographic disaster of dystopian magnitude is on our horizon, moving towards us, and sooner or later it'll slam into us. Population ageing and wealth inequality pose serious risks to a fair and equal future for all Australians. As a nation, we've chosen to look away. Perhaps it's too hard to think about. But the longer we look away, the less time we have to act.

Our politicians are particularly good at looking away, and persuading us to keep looking away, too. As I've noted already, they've become experts at finding ways to distract us, with their talk of congestion, crowded schools, long waiting times for hospital beds, and threats of terrorism. Politicians of all stripes attempt to misdirect our attention in this way, like waving sparklers in our faces to distract us from the searing bright asteroid hurtling towards us. Such distractions are not only unhelpful; they're actively harmful.

Political short-termism only compounds the problem. Electoral terms at the federal level have been around three to six months in the last ten years, despite the official three-year maximum for the House of Represent-atives, due to frequent changes to the federal leadership of the major parties. Priorities and policy inevitably tend to shift as a new leader takes on the prime ministership part way through the standard three-year term, even though the same party remains in government. These shifts inev-itably disrupt long-term funding plans, particularly plans for desperately needed infrastructure. But our future as a nation depends on long-term strategic thinking, planning and action. So how do we turn the challenges we're facing into opportunities? And what will it take for our politicians to work together across the political divide to get the hard stuff done?

Myth-busting and the unspoken issues

Population and immigration myths persist in Australian society. Experts, myself included, naively like to think that if we merely share the facts, people will listen and be convinced. It's not that simple, though. Australians are fearful. The world is changing, and so is the place we call home. Yet no matter what political or ideological camp we belong to, deep down we have the same interests at heart. We want our nation to be prosperous, and we want the riches enjoyed by current generations to be enjoyed by the generations to come. But this isn't going happen if we con-tinue along the course we're on. We need to recognise our common objectives first, so the debate can proceed from there.

The stoush between anti-vaxxers and pro-vaxxers offers an interesting parallel. Both sides have the same concern – children's wellbeing – but fear gets in the way. Science has failed us by allowing false data to be published on the harms of vaccinations, and as non-experts we're left to weigh up the details ourselves, without the knowledge we need to distinguish the good information from the bad. Under the circumstances, it's understandable that emotion ends up driving the debate, rather than facts. Once emotion is involved, though, facts are no longer enough. You can't persuade someone to take a different view of the problem when they're angry. The best approach in such cases is to try to identify a common objective. Common ground offers a new starting point and makes dialogue possible.

We need to take a similar approach in discussing Australia's future. Population matters need to be demystified, but information alone won't change minds. We have a common objective: to safeguard the future of the generations to come, at the same time promoting social wellbeing and a positive, harmonious culture. Once we've agreed on that, we can take another look at the facts and start working together to meet the challenges we're facing.

Immigration and innovation: Fighting future threats

In Australia, as in many parts of the world, we fear change perhaps more than anything else – particularly the change we see in our daily lives and our immediate environment. Successive governments have shown us that this fear can be a powerful driver: when they demonise migrants for political gain, it's our fear of change, of the unfamiliar, that they rely on. But when faced with the far more frightening spectre of climate change, they are paralysed by fear: our leaders' response has been one of denial and delay. If we're to survive as a nation, we need to get past our fear of change and confront it head on. Sometimes this means recognising there is no real threat; in other cases, it means recognising grave, even existential threats, and then acting anyway, refusing to give up hope.

Whether we like it or not, Australia is changing, and so is our climate. Those are facts we have to accept. But confronting fear isn't as scary or impossible as it sounds. One important step is to change the language we use to talk about these issues. Some might argue that it's actions, not words, that really matter. But it is words that shape our attitudes, and our attitudes determine our actions. The Australian political elite manufacture fear with negative language: terms like 'big Australia' and 'mass migration' are tossed about, fuelling an unhealthy and unproductive obsession with population size, yet the words 'big' and 'mass' are never defined. They naturally incite fear, giving the impression that population growth is out of control and that our numbers will continue to expand endlessly. But Australia's population isn't out of control and endlessly expanding. Nothing could be further from the truth. Meanwhile, the real issues that could in fact lead us to the brink of demographic disaster – an ageing population and falling birth rate – are overlooked. Accuracy matters.

A useful discussion requires honest language, not fearful hyperbole.

For similar reasons, the language we use to talk about climate needs to change too, but in this case we need to describe the problems we're facing in stronger terms, not more moderate ones. As I write this, in early January 2020, I can barely breathe; the air quality in Canberra right now is the worst in the world, due to the intense fires raging across the south-eastern states. Throughout the English-speaking world, it is becoming more and more common to talk of the 'climate crisis' or 'climate emergency', terms which quite rightly convey greater urgency than the carefully neutral 'climate change'. Meanwhile, Australia's current federal government, long reluctant to acknowledge climate change, speaks of it only grudgingly even now, under pressure from an angry public feeling betrayed by their leaders' inaction.

Another important step is to focus on the potential that change creates for innovation. When facing a crisis, it helps to remind ourselves that humans have survived enormous and even catastrophic change in the past and often emerged stronger as a result. Cast your mind all the way back to our discussion of demographic transitions. People and populations have been innovating since day dot. Without our ancestors' talent for innovation and adaptation, you and I wouldn't even be here, let alone communicating via the pages of a book.

Taking food as an example, it's easy to see how huge disruptions to the status quo have benefited humanity over time. The development of farming was one of the biggest changes that humans have ever experienced, radically altering the structure of many formerly nomadic societies as hunting and gathering were replaced by agriculture. As we saw in Chapter 1, this was true of some First Nations cultures in Australia, such as that of the Gunditjmara people, who built the Budj Bim eel traps in south-western Victoria, just as it was in other parts of the world. For these societies, farming was an answer to problems of scarcity and uncertainty.

Cooking was another innovation revolutionary in its impact, making many otherwise inedible or indigestible plant or animal foods both edible and digestible, at the same time killing pathogens and parasites and making nutrients easier to absorb. Cooking itself would later be revolutionised by technology, in the form of gas and electric stoves. The noxious gases produced by cooking over an open fire indoors can pose a serious health threat, causing respiratory difficulties and even fatalities – not to mention the risk of fire. In places not too far from Australia, including Indonesia, indoor cooking in the confined spaces of the home can still be deadly, but in wealthy countries, these problems have been resolved. Over the course of the past 200 years, humans have developed the know-how needed to make cooking safe, transforming the way we perform one of life's most basic activities to keep us safe and ensure our survival.

The way we feed the nation, and the world, has become even smarter and more efficient in recent years, too, again aided by innovation and technology. Pesticides and evidence-based approaches to farming have contributed to greater yields. Scientists have developed processes to make plants and livestock better adapted to the environments we live in. For example: agricultural scientists have identified genetic variations that make wheat plants vulnerable to a common disease, wheat rust, meaning that we know how and why it affects some and not all wheat plants.[1] Rather than using chemicals to protect crops against this disease, we can now identify and select disease-resistant seedlings. As a result of such advances, famine is no longer just a way of life.[2] And in areas where famines and conflict continue to ravage populations, innovative solutions can drastically reduce the loss of lives. Organisations like UNICEF now deliver life-saving nutrients to children vulnerable to severe malnutrition in a simple squeeze pouch containing a couple of teaspoons of high-protein nut paste. Consumed daily for around six weeks, this paste can mean the difference between life and death.[3] These pouches are revolutionising the response to famine.

But the production and consumption of food is just one example of how we've benefited from innovation. Technological advances have positively transformed our lives again and again over the centuries, with many significant changes taking place within living memory. Women, in particular, have benefited from innovation. I've already discussed the world of opportunity that opened to many women and girls with the automation of housework and the improved variety, reliability and availability of birth control, but access to education and employment aren't the only benefits Australian women have gained over the past fifty years. We're much less likely to die in childbirth now, for example, and we're living longer, too. Technological innovations have contributed enormously to improvements in life expectancy at birth, and to better health generally. Immunisations have seen infant mortality rates hit historical lows and helped to increase the likelihood of newborns surviving to their first and subsequent birthdays. Anaesthetics, improved surgical techniques and greater understanding of health and disease, including the social determinants of health, have led to more effective means of treatment of ill health.[4]

Women and children have seen the greatest gains, but men, too, are living longer, healthier lives due to innovation and new technologies. Improved safety in the workplace, via technological advances in machinery and operations, has seen industrial death rates decline drastically. These changes particularly affect men, more so than women. Social and cultural expectations have changed too, such that workplace fatalities are no longer considered an unavoidable part of doing business, which has in turn lead to further improvements in occupational health and safety. The benefits aren't felt only by workers; greater workplace safety has led to greater efficiencies in the way industries operate, and therefore greater productivity.

The message here is that innovation has always been the solution to our problems in the past, and it will be the solution to our current and future problems too. These problems may seem insurmountable, but I have faith in human ingenuity. Challenges present us with opportunities to innovate. Let's look at food again, as an example. The globalisation of food production and consumption certainly poses challenges. Global forces undermine food security in individual nations, especially poorer ones. We're also transporting food over longer and longer distances, racking up what are known as 'food miles', at considerable cost to the environment. Both of these issues are cause for concern, but they also offer opportunities to innovate. Crops can be transported over long distances much more efficiently than livestock, so we might try adapting to a diet that includes less meat, for example, and find more effective ways to use pastoral land that will supply greater numbers of people with protein.[5] One thing is certain: reducing consumption of meat would not only be good for our environment but also for Australians' health.

The biggest challenge we're facing is the climate crisis, which poses genuine and extremely serious threats to our population's health and wellbeing. While politicians and other commentators are still squabbling about whether climate change is real, scientists have come to a consensus: it's real, humans have contributed to it, and the world is in grave danger from its effects. In fact, according to a survey of published research papers, over 97 per cent of scientists believe that climate change is real and humans are the cause.[6]

Australia is especially vulnerable to climate change. The fires that devastated the south-eastern states early in

2020 are the most obvious proof of this, but our vulnerability goes far beyond our exposure to longer, hotter, drier summers. Recall the location of the majority of the population along the coast. Rising seas already lap at coastal housing in some parts of Australia, and this problem will only get worse.[7] But it's not just people living near the coast who are at risk. Urban design and the distribution of socio-economically vulnerable people across Australian cities and towns pose further challenges. Take Penrith, a thriving suburb in Sydney's outer west. Penrith is considered a good place to establish a home and family while still being within commuting distance from the city centre. Housing is more affordable than in areas closer to the city, and Penrith's greater open space lends itself to a more laid-back lifestyle. Temperatures in Penrith are typically hotter than they are on the coast, though. The overall average annual difference is around 3 degrees Celsius, but this average hides the starker extremes experienced in summer.[8] The days there can be unbearably hot, and the nights not much better. This has always been the case, but things are getting worse. On 4 January 2020, as I was working on this chapter, Penrith was one of the hottest places on earth, with a record-breaking maximum temperature of 48.9 degrees Celsius.[9]

The demographics of the area compound the problem, leaving the people of Penrith more vulnerable than the average. Penrith isn't a wealthy area, and adapting housing to accommodate climate extremes is expensive. There are costs involved in insulating a home, planting tree cover or installing and running an air conditioner, to name just a few of the usual options. It's no surprise that on extraordinarily hot days the people there flock to shopping centres to stay cool. Their homes just don't offer the protection they need from the heat. Hot days followed by hot nights give little opportunity for recovery, putting those with chronic illness and the very young, very old and very poor at particular risk. Deaths spike during prolonged heatwaves, after days and nights of sustained high temperatures.[10] People's lives are literally at risk, and it's only going to get worse.

But where is the action? While the country burns, Australians are still fighting over whether climate change is real. Instead, we like to tell ourselves that immigration and population are the problems. Interestingly, the likes of Pauline Hanson are extremely vocal about their belief that human-induced climate change is a hoax, yet their concern for the environment suddenly comes to the fore when they're advocating for cuts to immigration. Yes, climate change is in part the result of a growing global population, but we can't undo its effects by cutting immigration. Fewer people migrating to Australia won't change the overall size of the world's population. People still exist, whether they're living in Beijing or Sydney. We need to adapt our behaviour, not limit our numbers. We must try to slow the rate of climate change, and stop it, if we can, but we also need to find ways to live with the change we are already experiencing.

Australians are natural inventors and entrepreneurs, so there's no doubt we'll figure something out. This is the birthplace of wi-fi, the Hills hoist and cask wine, after all.[11] It's not necessarily about making drastic changes. Innovation is sometimes about being smarter and more effective – doing the same things, but in more efficient ways. To futureproof our country, we'll need to invest in infrastructure – not just the physical stuff, like housing and community supports, but also less tangible things, like health and education – and to back it up, we'll need good policy. That's where demographers come in, but more on that later.

Australia isn't headed for a Malthusian catastrophe: we won't drain the country dry and starve to death. We're innovators, and innovators thrive in a crisis. The demographic and climate crises we're facing are a double whammy, but I'm confident we'll rise to the challenge. It's time to get past our fear of change – to embrace immigration wholeheartedly, making the most of the new perspectives it brings, and to find new and better ways to live together on this oldest and driest of continents. It's time to stop clinging to the past, to give up the myth of a 'white Australia', and turn to a better, more inclusive future.

Overcoming the white Australia mentality

Whether we like it or not, recognise it or not, the white Australia policy is still with us today. It's unspoken these days, no longer official, but it's still there. White Australia endures on the playground and the streets, in boardrooms and in parliament, in history books, on social media, and over the dinner table in homes across the country. Fear of the other, whether conscious or unconscious, forms the foundation of Australian society.

In an evolutionary sense, such fears are designed to keep us safe. Our primate ancestors were wary of anyone outside their immediate group, and this suspicion served them well, helping them to survive and pass on their genes. In some ways this impulse still serves us well – we are careful to protect our children from anyone we don't know, for example, until we are sure we can trust them, thereby ensuring the survival of our own genetic line. But at a broader social level, this trait no longer confers any advantage. Our distrust of those from other countries or cultures won't help us to survive – it's more likely to doom us to extinction.

We've already discussed the fact that Australia needs migrants in order to survive. Here are a couple more facts: migrants aren't the enemy, and they aren't bringing terrorism to our shores. Homegrown terrorism is the real problem: some right-wing locals in predominantly white European countries get worked up about non-European migration, fearing they'll be displaced by newcomers to their country, and the most extreme among them sometimes react to these fears with violence.[12] It's not about competition for jobs and resources in these cases but something more visceral. Threats to their majority status make these people fear for the perceived 'purity' of their society, culture and race. Our leaders have not done enough to address the growth of this form of extremism; in some cases, they even pander to these people. Australia's demand-driven, skills-based migration program is the means by which our economy stays afloat, but our politicians often seek to problematise immigration for political gain. First they invent a problem where there is none, then they appease voters by offering a 'solution' to that problem. The whole exercise is nothing more than a fantastic play of political pageantry.

Australian politicians tend to view immigration somewhat ambivalently. It is either good and bad, or – paradoxically – good and bad all at once. This duality is somewhat perplexing, yet it allows them to appeal to people on both sides of the argument. It's like an internal conversation: 'Yes, immigration has benefits, but, no, it's not for us.' It isn't all that different to the often-heard: 'I'm not racist, but …' This is evident in the public discourse around population growth and population change. The so-called problems caused by population growth would not merely disappear if we received fewer migrants or even no migrants. Australia's population would continue to grow even if immigration were to stop altogether. As we have seen, the cities with the biggest inflow of overseas migrants – Melbourne, Sydney and Brisbane – will continue to see population growth in the medium term even without any migrant intake.

Across the world, social and cultural arguments against immigration are increasingly intertwined with environmental objections to population growth. But rarely is anything said – certainly not in Australia – about restricting natural increase. It is a sensitive question, especially where white European majorities are involved. At a demographic conference in Budapest attended by representatives of far-right organisations and high-profile opponents of immigration, former Liberal prime minister Tony Abbott advocated for a higher local birth rate yet greater control over immigration. Abbott told his audience that the 'real extinction rebellion' movement needed is 'not against our failure to reduce emissions ... but against our failure to produce more children'.[13] Further, Abbott stated that the greatest threat to the western world was 'sustained decline in the birth rate', rather than global warming or terrorism. Statements such as Abbott's invoke what has come to be known as the 'great replacement' – the idea that dominant peoples and cultures are being replaced by outsider or minority peoples and cultures. In Australia, as in many parts of the world, the fear is that people of Islamic faith will eventually outnumber the non-Muslim white majority.

The threat of non-white migrant groups overtaking local white majorities is a baseless and extremely harmful myth, one which doesn't seem to go away, despite the solid evidence against it. (There's no way people of Islamic faith could become a majority in Australia, short of mass religious conversion. It certainly won't happen through births or immigration.)[14] Yet politicians such as Fraser Anning have used this claim to stir up anxiety, even panic, in the general population. It's this unfounded and irrational fear that motivates mass killers such as the Australian man who attacked two suburban mosques in Christchurch, New Zealand, in March 2019.[15] The killer, a white male from regional New South Wales, identified as a white suprema-cist. A self-declared 'eco-fascist', he believed that Muslims, as a minority group, were the cause of environmental deg-radation. He massacred 51 people in their place of wor-ship, and wounded 49.[16]

No matter what you choose to call them – eco-fascists, eco-nativists or environmental eugenicists – people who share this man's views are part of a new movement journalist Susie Cagle has identified as seeking to 'green-wash racism'.[17] A typical argument put forward by these types is that Australia shouldn't welcome immigrants from less developed countries, because when migrants arrive from, say, India, they're likely to adopt the lifestyle of the Australian population, increasing their individual carbon footprint. Such a policy would clearly entrench the privi-lege already enjoyed by those in wealthy countries, giving preference to migrants from other wealthy countries while disadvantaging potential migrants from poorer countries. I see such arguments being put forward all the time, espe-cially in the comments sections beneath articles I publish about the benefits of immigration.

The nativists' insistence that the interests of the local population be protected above all others sounds reason-able – of course we should be looking after our own – but such policies come at a cost, particularly for migrants already contributing to a nation and hoping to become a part of it. We often speak of assimilation, of migrants' obligation to adopt Australian customs and values. The problem is it's near impossible to become the ideal 'new

Australian' when the locals won't let you forget you're not one of the team. Migrants are always seen as the other, never good enough because of their birthplace, and constantly asked to prove their 'Australian-ness'. Politicians encourage these attitudes. Some recent prime ministers – John Howard, Julia Gillard and Tony Abbott – have used nativism as a means of gaining popular support. For Howard it was *Tampa* and terrorism; for Gillard it was 'local jobs first;[18] and Abbott spruiked immigration for economic gain but bemoaned the arrival of 'boat people'.[19] Our current prime minister, Scott Morrison, won the top job due at least in part to the reputation for toughness he'd established as minister for immigration and border protection.

Though it's no longer official policy, eugenics still lurks at the heart of our national politics, fundamental to our ideas about race and identity, just as it was to the white Australia policy. Australia regularly faces questions about its allegiances to countries in the region versus countries further afield, and our answers are revealing. As a nation, we've typically aligned ourselves with similar-looking nations, literally choosing our allies on face value. Australia has whitewashed its First Nations history, and some of us want to greenwash the present, seeking to shore up the idea that we're a remote outpost of Europe. Don't get me wrong – I like Eurovision as much as the next nerd. But Australia isn't European. Our future lies elsewhere.

The paradox in all of this is that Australia is a world leader when it comes to multiculturalism. But the shackles of white Australia aren't easily removed. In the mainstream media, discussion of congestion in our major cities is often accompanied by images of non-European faces packed in trains or along railway platforms. These images imply what the articles hint at without saying explicitly: that migrants are the cause of our problems. Whether we consciously recognise what's being implied doesn't matter. We're still taking in the message at some level. It goes to show just how deep the effects of the long-abolished white Australia policy really go. It's difficult to shake the weight of the past, but it must be done. It takes leadership. And showing leadership is damned hard, especially when you also want to be popular. Just ask contemporary Australian political leaders.

Again, language matters here. Small changes in the way we talk about immigration and multiculturalism can make a huge difference. For example, referring to people who migrate to Australia as 'imports' must stop. Terms like this undermine migrants' humanity, inviting the listener to view them as commodities rather than people. Calling migrants 'job thieves' has to stop too. It's simply not true, and the perpetuation of this myth threatens the cohesion of our society. Australia is a highly successful multicultural country; we should be proud of that fact and really let it shine. Politicians, particularly those in the major parties, have a particularly important role to play in changing the way these conversations are framed, along with other public figures such as journalists and social commentators, but we can all do our part.

As individuals, we can certainly hold others account-able for their speech, refusing to accept intolerant and inflammatory language. This can be done respectfully, to create the possibility for dialogue – I recommend taking the same approach you'd use to correct a child using improper grammar or pronunciation. Start by repeating the words they've used back to them, and then rephrase, correcting the false assumption or derogatory language. For example, if someone said that immigrants steal local jobs, I'd say, 'Steal local jobs? Fill jobs we can't fill, more like it.' I'd finish by saying something like 'It's migrants who keep us afloat, and I'm so grateful that they want to come here.' You might end up in an argument, but you never know. You might just change someone's mind by sharing the facts with them.

Australia has clung to an outdated idea of itself in an attempt to stave off outside influence or threat – but the greatest threat we face now is from the lingering effects of the white Australia policy and a fearful mentality that sees us looking inwards instead of outwards. Australians aren't ever likely to agree on a specific population trajectory or immigration intake. Nor would we want total agreement – difference of opinion is a defining characteristic of a free society. But the one thing we likely can all agree on is that Australia needs to get smart about its future. Population waits for no one. Population is something that just happens, regardless of our best intentions, as history has shown. However, as I hope I've made clear by now, we kinda know which way we're headed. It's time to flip ahead through the pages of this Choose Your Own Adventure story. If we take a peek at the potential outcomes, we can decide which one looks the most appealing and then figure out the path we'll take to get there.

CONCLUSION

Demography needs a makeover

When I say that demography needs a makeover, I mean two things. First, Australia's demography needs a make-over: we need to find a way to keep the average age of the population down, at the same time creating a fairer, more equal society. But the discipline of demography itself also needs a makeover, if demographers are going to do our part to help the nation achieve its full potential. I'm going to wrap up now by telling you what I think we need to do if Australia, and my chosen profession, are going to survive and thrive.

It's within our power to plan, prepare for and respond to changes in population. The problem is Australia hasn't really seen planning of this kind necessary. Since our last earnest attempt a population policy, in the years after World War II, we've made several half-hearted and whole-hearted efforts, all of which have failed, some quite terri-bly. For the most part, though, we've just overlooked the question altogether. Even during the postwar era, Aus-tralia didn't really plan or enact sensible policy to support the population of the future, focusing instead on growth targets. Harried population plans made prior to the 2019 federal election were more or less purely aesthetic, designed to appease anti-immigration sentiment on the part of the general public. The 40-page plan was more glossy prospectus than the real thing, vague on details and featuring more graphics than serious strategy.[1] Possibly the only real news in it was the announcement that a population centre would be established to inform and direct sensible policy, but the devil was in the detail: the government planned to plonk this new centre within Treasury – a federal government department – rather than making it an independent body.[2]

The plan focused on the connection between immigration and congestion, and, to a lesser extent, how Australia could help migrants better assimilate and how the government bottom line might derive greater benefit from immigration. It didn't have much to say about the other parts of the demographic equation: births and deaths. Women and families in particular got shafted. Even more revealing was the emphasis on regional settlement: pushing new migrants out to the regions. The federal government went so far as redefining the term 'regional area', even categorising Canberra, the national capital, as such. For me, as a demographer, the most alarming thing about this plan was that the rhetoric wasn't matched by funding commitments. Policymakers seemed intent on recreating past mistakes, assuming that regional areas already had the infrastructure needed to house migrants. Regional settlement policies have never worked in Australia: once new migrants have served their time in the regions, they typically move on. And where do they move on to? Areas with education and employment opportunities. This is an important lesson for population planners: social and economic infrastructure are vital if a policy is to succeed.

We want a population policy, and we need a population policy – but it has to be one that works. So how do we go about it? A formal inquiry isn't necessary or even desirable. The last one we had was long, expensive and resulted in nothing more than a massive wad of words, albeit good ones, which went to waste. What we need is to talk to and hear from interested members of the public. But despite what Pauline Hanson has proposed, no, a population action plan shouldn't be put to a public vote. Population policy is far too complex and multifaceted for a simple yes/no plebiscite. Moreover, policy by populism is lazy and lacks rigour. Just because something might get a political party elected doesn't make it a good idea. And we shouldn't be motivated purely by economic concerns; the wellbeing of the population should determine our choices. Research, evidence and expert advice need to take centre stage as we put together our policy framework. The experts won't always agree, and neither will interpretations of the evidence, but that's okay.

Good population policy takes into account complex social issues that are the purview of numerous government departments. Every ministerial portfolio, from education and training to health, welfare and even defence, deals with questions of population in one way or another, meaning that policy must take a whole-of-government approach.

Research exploring how to approach complex policy issues indicates that 'joined-up government' is the best way to address difficult social problems about which there is little agreement, in order to overcome the 'silo' mentality of government departments.[3] Consultation must take place not just between federal government silos but up and down and between state and territory governments as well. The reason that most recent attempts at population policy in Australia have been unsuccessful might be that a coordinated approach is necessary but has never been attempted, let alone achieved. It's simply been too hard. That, or perhaps politicians' reluctance to make hard decisions which might mean risking their re-election.

I know none of this will be easy – I'm not that much of an optimist. Ministers, even within the same political party, will never agree on everything, least of all how to deal with population change. Developing such a policy would require commitment and flexibility across numerous governmental departments and organisations. The effort required to coordinate the policy creation process and its subsequent implementation might be enough to see the project shelved before it was even started – but surely it's worth a go?

'Innovation narratives' are one technique we might use to move beyond territorial and ideological spats and into action.[4] Such narratives are essentially a form of storytelling, designed to get people used to the idea of change. For example, imagine you work for a local council and you're going to introduce a green waste bin to the regular curb-side garbage collection, alongside the rubbish bin and recycling bin that residents are already familiar with. Introducing a third bin might seem excessive and could potentially be confusing, but there's solid evidence to support making this change. The introduction of the green waste bin will save the council money and has environmental benefits too: there will be less waste going to landfill, and food scraps and leaf litter from the new bin will be turned into mulch and then sold. To get locals residents on board, you decide to run an advertising campaign. The innovation narrative forms the centre of your campaign, telling the story behind the coming change so that residents will have time to get used to the idea. In your advertising materials, you announce that a new bin will be delivered soon, setting out its benefits and explaining what its arrival will mean for residents in practical terms (such as what kind of waste to put in it, and which night to put it out on the curb). The point is to create a feeling of community, a sense that everyone is working together towards a common goal. Though the scope of our project is vastly more complex, the same techniques could be used to frame and progress the debate as we work towards a population policy, with fairness, sustainability and the greatest possible wellbeing for all as our common goal.

The current short-sighted approach to politics and policy at the federal, state and territory levels of government will need to be addressed, so it won't get in the way of the kind of long-term investment needed to fund major reform and development. This might perhaps be achieved through a more bipartisan approach, or a reimagining of the way political terms are structured and infrastructure is built. The intergenerational wealth inequality angle might be the necessary 'in' to get the conversation started. We can all agree it's a problem that homeownership is out of reach of many young Australians. It may alter the manner in which young people form relationships and families, which could, if they delay having children, result in fewer children being born overall, further exacerbating the adverse consequences of an ageing population.

A coordinated approach to policy development, funding, investment and practice is necessary to ensure future generations experience the same way of life that we enjoy today – if not a better one. This necessarily means a cradle-to-grave approach to policy and practice. For example, the children of today and tomorrow are the workforce of the future. Sufficient government investment is required – particularly in health and education – for babies to have a good start in life. This means providing adequate housing; welfare support for families; high-quality education for all, no matter where they may live in Australia; and accessible and affordable healthcare. What we need is an actual fair go, not just a rhetorical one.

Remember the ovarian lottery? The idea that you're either born lucky or you're not? That's our current reality. But inequality need not be a life sentence. We can use the idea of the 'ladder of life' (see figure on following page) as a basis for policy, taking measures to ensure that everyone starts on the same rung, and that they're given a leg-up whenever they need it, so that we all have the chance to climb as high as we like.

If education is the passport to life, let's start there. The habits and behaviours established when we're young typically continue and develop over time, so it stands to reason that preschool be the first step up on the ladder, a way to counter the inequalities already present even before kids get to school. Quality school experiences for three- to five-year-olds can be an equaliser, giving kids the boost they need to reach the next rungs: primary and secondary school. Preschool can help children from all backgrounds to feel comfortable in educational environments, and to develop attitudes, habits and behaviours that promote learning, social engagement and interpersonal trust, supplementing their parents' efforts at home. Properly funded preschool education gives children from socioeconomically disadvantaged families opportunities that other children are already able to take advantage of – a leg-up on the ladder of life.

A robust education system would grant access to schooling – and post-school education and training – of the same quality to every child, regardless of their family's postcode or socioeconomic circumstances. One of the goals of our education system must be to provide the nation with the best possible workforce in future years. Australia lacks the workforce we need to deal with our current demographic situation, let alone the one we're marching towards. At present we address this lack through immigration, but that's only part of the long-term solution.

The ladder of life

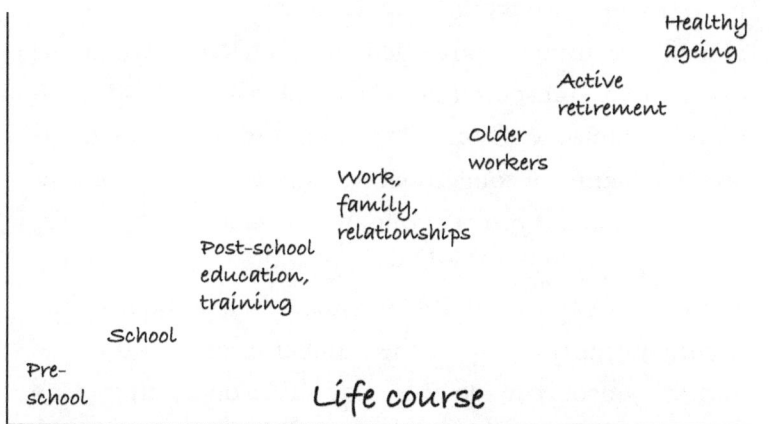

Healthy
ageing

Active
retirement

Older
workers

Work,
family,
relationships

Post-school
education,
training

School

Pre-
school

Life course

We might not agree with nativist rhetoric that puts local workers first, but we can all agree that investing in local education and training is not just desirable but fundamental to our future prosperity.

How we work also needs to change. (No, robots won't take our jobs, by the way. Or at least not all of them.) As the population ages, the government will push for greater productivity and full participation in the labour force. Balancing work, relationships, childcare and leisure is likely to become more difficult as a result, with consequences for workers' physical and mental health. This will impact women far more than men, unless our approach to gender and equality in the workplace and social attitudes more broadly don't undergo enormous change. The health of the workforce is vital, so we'll need to find ways to cope with these changing demands. Thinking about where we live might be a useful place to begin: how near or far is it from where we work, shop, or interact socially? Could any of these things be arranged more conveniently or done differently? Transportation is just one part of the pie, but an important one. Once we've all agreed that immigrants aren't to blame for congestion, we can start looking for genuine solutions. If you're sitting in peak-hour traffic, you're part of the problem. Could we adjust the traditional nine-to-five hours to ease traffic pressures? What about reducing the number of trips – the number of cars on the road and the journeys made every day? Telecommuting could be a major solution here. We need to do whatever we can to make life less stressful for future generations.

Addressing the generational divide will be important too. Conflict over which generation has it worst has become common in the media, and it's increasingly common in political discourse, too. Boomers fight it out with their kids and grandkids, each generation claiming they've had the toughest time of it. The baby boomers resent the implication that they had an easy ride, arguing that they've worked hard all their lives and have earned their success. But research shows that while their generation experienced their own set of issues, younger generations have definitely got it worse. Throughout history, a social compact has been observed: younger generations provide for older generations when they are no longer able to support themselves. And provide they have. But since the introduction of compulsory superannuation, this compact has been broken: we now save for our own retirement rather than supporting others as they age. Baby boomers are better able to look after themselves financially in old age than any generation before them, but this is, as always, down to luck: they were born at the right time. We need to look at that ladder of life again, and adjust our policy settings accordingly. It's not extravagant spending that stops younger people from buying their own homes. As discussed in Chapter 4, it's policies that favour older generations at their expense. As active participants in the labour force, they are, after all, funding the nation, so we need to do a better job of looking after them.

Attempts to bridge the generational divide have to go both ways, though. Older people face barriers to full participation in many areas of life, and their contributions are frequently undervalued, particularly in the workplace. Older workers possess fundamental skills and knowledge, yet Australia's support for them is woeful, especially when it comes to protecting them from discrimination. The wealthy (politicians among them) have much greater control over how long they'll continue to work and what kind of work they'll do as they age. For most of us, though, employment becomes less reliable and predictable as we age, and our choices become more limited, due in part to workplace attitudes to older people. At present, older Australians face enormous discrimination in the workplace. This is definitely something we'll need to address, as is the fact that our social security safety nets aren't all that flash.

Retirement is, of course, a lovely thing to consider. Ah ... But in reality, it's a complicated proposition. For many young people, retirement may never truly happen – not full retirement, anyhow. Older people may find they need to work past the point at which they feel ready to retire, because they can't afford it yet, or they may be made redundant and have trouble getting a new job, despite being willing and able to carry on working. And even when people do retire, whether wholly or partially, they don't cease to be important to the economy. Volunteering, becoming a trainer or mentoring younger people are just some ways that retirees can continue to contribute while also maintaining valuable social contact. This is particularly important where retirees don't have family as a social support.

Active retirement helps to support healthy ageing. Appropriate, affordable, well-situated housing is vital here. We need to support older people to 'age in place', remaining in the family home as long as they wish to, but other options, such as retirement villages, also need greater levels of support to provide high-quality care. The cost of retrofitting an existing home or moving to a new home so that older people can live comfortably must be factored into our plan, and should be available in every community. The physical proximity of older people to their long-established social connections has a huge impact on their health and wellbeing, and moving away can cause unnecessary stress. New approaches to housing for retirees and empty-nesters could also help address housing affordability for younger people.

A cradle-to-grave approach to population policy would see older people as important human investments, worth protecting – assets worth exploiting to their fullest. If people are given the benefit of high-quality education, training and health care throughout their lives, their well-being as they age will be greatly improved. This would reduce health-care costs in their later years, and would also allow them to work longer if they wished to, as many do. Both of these benefits – reduced health-care costs and longer working lives – would relieve at least part of the burden carried by younger generations. This is a long-term game we're playing here, but the gains we make along the way will continue to pay off long into the future. Everyone gets older, and if you're not old yet, you will be one day – so we all stand to benefit from policies that lead to healthier ageing.

But where exactly do births, deaths and migration fit in this new population policy, I hear you ask. Good question. Once again, our main goal is population well-being. Let's start by looking at the birth rate. If families have secure housing and material resources, they will be able to have more children, if they want to, guaranteeing a larger workforce in the years to come. Others will still choose to have small families, or to have no children at all, so overseas immigration will continue to be necessary. We will need a balanced, demand-driven, skills-based migration program, with an intake around the size Australians are already accustomed to. In Chapter 5 we looked at what might happen if immigration were to stop or be reduced and learned that life would be a hell of a lot harder without the vital contributions migrants make to Australian society. And as for deaths, well, a cradle-to-grave population policy would mean fairer, healthier lives, meaning fairer, healthier ageing, meaning healthier, more active older people and fewer premature deaths due to poor-quality or inadequate health care.

Underpinning all this is one fundamental idea: accessibility. Accessible means appropriate, available, affordable and easily accessed. Accessibility is essential to a fairer society, whether we're talking about education, employment, health care, housing, or any of life's basics. Ultimately, this is a question of infrastructure – both the tangible stuff like trains and trams and schools and public pools, and the stuff you can't see but rely on anyway, stuff that holds us together as a society, like laws and systems and processes. But to ensure that these things are accessible, we have to consider more abstract questions, such as gender, disability, diversity and the needs of people in rural and regional communities. That might mean funding programs that encourage girls to study STEM subjects in high school, for example, or providing English classes for new migrants. It could mean subsidising essential services in the bush, or retrofitting public buildings to make them accessible to people in wheelchairs. It might mean anything at all, in fact, that breaks down barriers to full social and economic participation for all of us. A fairer Australia means *everyone* comes along for the ride, and accessibility for all is paramount.

In Australia, gender inequality in the workplace and in the home isn't usually a consideration in the development of population policy. Yet the question of gender is fundamental to population wellbeing. The gendered division of domestic labour has changed a great deal in my lifetime. Like my mother, I have a large family – she had eight kids, I have seven – but her life as a young wife and mother was very different to mine today. As I explained earlier, Mum resigned from her job when she married my father, and from that point on she was responsible for running the household, while Dad did paid work outside the home. My partner, on the other hand, is our children's primary carer. We juggle our contributions to the family based on our strengths and likes, rather than our genders. Households like ours are becoming more common, but they're not yet the norm. Australian men do more housework now than they used to, but in most Australian families it is still women who do the heavy lifting, domestically speaking.[5] This is especially the case when it comes to raising children – which is hard work, and also crucial to the future functioning of our society.

I have an intimate knowledge of the problems families with children experience in juggling work and other responsibilities, so I've given serious thought to how things could be done differently. Families who need or want support from the community should be entitled to more, as should parents who want the opportunity to balance paid work with caring for children or other family members. Greater childcare subsidies through family support payments are one way in which the government could easily intervene to promote family and child wellbeing for future prosperity.

I can't pretend to know anywhere near as much about disability or diversity policy, or the problems faced by Australians living in remote communities, so I'll leave it to others to address those questions. Similarly, it's not up to me, as a white European Australian, to talk about how to address the ongoing damage done by the dispossession of First Nations people and the White Australia policy. It's clear, though, that any population strategy for Australia's future must address our history of racism, which has been with us since the British first arrived and continues to the present day right throughout the country. White Australia's fear of the other has always been a threat to First Nations people and is still a threat today. Migrant communities face similar threats, with Muslims in particular singled out as 'un-Australian'. All I'll say here is that I'm a big believer in listening to the people who'll be affected by a new policy before deciding which path we should take when we're standing at a fork in the road and peering at the distant horizon.

Another huge and very important subject that I'll mention only in passing is that of environmental sustainability. The mandated adoption of environmentally sustainable practices by Australian businesses is long overdue, and any contemporary population policy for Australia would have to give this serious consideration. Land use, water consumption and management of other natural resources would also need serious consideration, as would food security.

There's just one last question I'd like to address before

I give you my ten-point plan for the future of us, and that's population size. A lot of people, including politicians like Pauline Hanson, among others, have publicly called for limits to population growth. Others have called for official targets, hoping to swell the population to a specific size. But neither caps nor targets are needed, and they could potentially have frightening consequences. When governments seek to dictate how many people may or may not live in a certain community, or how many children they can have, there is a risk that coercive measures will be brought to bear, as when First Nations Australians were forced to leave their homelands, or Chinese women were involuntarily subjected to abortions under their country's one-child policy. Where people choose to live and work and how many children they have is no one's business but their own. Once these things become a matter of public policy, our individual freedom is lost. Attempts to define optimal population size or carrying capacity are pointless anyway, because these figures are constantly growing as we discover innovative new techniques and technologies that allow us to do more with less. It's like trying to hit a moving target.

For me, this is a personal question, as well as a public policy question. You'd be surprised by the number of comments I've received over the years from friends and strangers alike, telling me I should consider abortion to limit the number of children I have, or the innumerable times some smart-arse has joked, 'Haven't you worked out how pregnancy happens yet?' These comments are hurtful – they insult my intelligence and capabilities, and undermine my identity as a mother. I like to tell people I enjoy sex too much, so I can watch them squirm, but really I want to tell them to shut up and to keep their nose out of my bedroom! My children are my hope for the future. If I can't see equality realised in my lifetime, I hope that they will, and I'll know that in the stories I've told them and the things I've taught them, I will have contributed to that change.

In the end, the most effective population policy for Australia is one that places population squarely at the centre of all policymaking and funding processes, so that it is seen as the natural starting point in any discussion of plans for our national future. Clear communication and respectful debate will be vital as we seek common ground from which to set out, and evidence will be our guide as we choose our path. Making it to the horizon will be no mean feat, but I have faith in us. It's going to be an adventure, but we're all in it together. I want to find out what happens next in the story of us, and if you've read on this far, I bet you do too.

As a demographer, it's my job to help draw up the map that we'll follow into the future. Without a coherent, integrated population policy, Australia risks going backwards. If you'd like to know exactly what my ideal population policy for Australia might look like, here's my ten-point plan:

1 Take a whole-of-government, joined-up approach to population.
2 Adopt a cradle-to-grave approach to population policy, breaking down policy and governmental silos.
3 Identify core policy areas, assign clear responsibilities to individual ministers and allocate guaranteed funding.
4 Rank infrastructure projects and investments in order of priority, determined by need, and publish budgets and time frames for every project in a format easily understood by the general public.
5 Communicate population strategy clearly to as wide an audience as possible, using innovation narratives and presenting Australia as a global citizen, not a lone island.
6 Issue a regular 'report card' tracking specific socioeconomic indicators, and link the allocation of funding to the achievement of set milestones.
7 Support research seeking innovative ways to guarantee food and water security and promote environmental sustainability.
8 Invest in national and state-based data infrastructure to guarantee evidence-based practices and policy.
9 Establish an independent centre for population to oversee and inform population policy.
10 Agree on a set term, longer than that of political election cycles, for the implementation and review of a non-partisan 'population plan'.

I said early on that demography is like a superpower, and it is. It freed me from the life of hardship I thought I was destined to endure. It made me realise that I counted, that I am more than the circumstances of my birth. I tell my children that demography got me out of the gutter. Without my serendipitous discovery of demography, I would have dropped out of university, narrowing my prospects and theirs. Demography gave me the language and skills to agitate and advocate for change – change that will have a real and positive impact within my lifetime.

But as much as I love it, demography needs a makeover. As demographers say, it's what you count that matters – and what we're counting needs to change. How we count it needs to change too. We need a wider focus, incorporating men in our analyses as well as women when we ask questions about everything from fertility to caring and work-life balance. Women must be seen as more than procreators and carers, or extra bodies to make up the shortfall in the labour market. We also need a greater diversity of voices, both within the academy and in the research community. To give you an idea of just how male the study of demography is in Australia, consider that no woman had been promoted to professor of demography at any Australian university until 2017, when Heather Booth received this recognition.

As always, I'm optimistic – Heather's work, along with that of others such as Edith Gray, Genevieve Heard, Ann Evans and Rebecca Kippen, has paved the way for a new wave of demographers. This new generation has studied with the greats, men like Peter McDonald, and they are now working hard to give our discipline the long-overdue makeover it needs. They include a diverse bunch of people who bring with them a wide range of life experiences and research interests. Tom Wilson is developing more accurate and flexible population projection techniques. Amina Keygan is investigating male fertility, helping to redress the current narrow focus on women. Brendan Churchill is conducting much needed work on the gig economy, and is also a pioneer in the move towards greater diversity in the categorisation of data relating to gender and sex. Alice Falkiner's exploration of multi-carers, aka the sandwich generation, has begun the work needed to acknowledge the role of women caring for children and elderly parents at the same time. Ariane Utomo works on understanding achieving gender equality in the home and workforce. Work by Tom, Amina, Brendan, Alice, Ariane and others like them will lay the foundations for genuine change in Australian society. Demography's voice is no longer exclusively white, male and privileged, and I'm excited to be part of that change.

My children may have lost the ovarian lottery, just like I did, but I work every day to create a new world for them, and for the frightened young Liz I still catch a glimpse of in the mirror every now and then. I want no other child to experience the feeling that they are less than anyone else, excluded from society. I wear my demographer's cape with pride, and I will keep fighting for a future where each and every one of us is equal.

Notes

Chapter 1 – How we got here: The peopling of Australia

1   Kaneda, T. and C. Haub (2018), How many people have ever lived on earth? <www.prb.org/howmanypeoplehaveeverlivedonearth>.

2   OECD, (2018) *A Broken Social Elevator? How to Promote Social Mobility. How Does Australia Compare?* <www.oecd.org/australia/social-mobililty-2018-AUS-EN.pdf>.

3   ABS (2018) *Life Tables States, Territories and Australia, 2015-2017.* Cat. No. 3302.0.55.001. Canberra.

4   Weeks, J.R. (2014) *Population: An introduction to the concepts and issues.* 12th edition. Boston: Cengage Learning.

5   Australian Research Council Centre of Excellence for Australian Biodiversity (2017), *Rewriting History: Australia's oldest known campsite*, <epicaustralia.org.au/rewriting-history-australias-oldest-known-campsite>.

6   Bradshaw, C., S. Ulm, A. Williams, M. Bird, R. Roberts, Z. Jacobs, F. Laviano, L. Weyrich, T. Friedrich, K. Norman, and F. Saltre (2019) 'Minimum founding populations for the first peopling of Sahul', *Nature: Ecology and Evolution,* 3/July: 1057–1063.

7   Bradshaw, C., S. Ulm, A. Williams, M. Bird, R. Roberts, Z. Jacobs, F. Laviano, L. Weyrich, T. Friedrich, K. Norman, and F. Saltre (2019) 'Minimum founding populations for the first peopling of Sahul', *Nature: Ecology and Evolution,* 3/July: 1057–1063.

8   Gammage, B. (2011) *The Biggest Estate on Earth: How Aborigines made Australia,* Allen & Unwin: Sydney.

9   Gammage, B. (2011) *The Biggest Estate on Earth: How Aborigines made Australia,* Allen & Unwin: Sydney.

10   McNiven, I. (2017) 'The detective work behind the Budj Bim eel traps World Heritage bid', The Conversation, 8 February, <theconversation.com/the-detective-work-behind-the-budj-bim-eel-traps-world-heritage-bid-71800>.

11   Builth, H. (2014) *Ancient Aboriginal Aquaculture Rediscovered: The archaeology of an Australian Cultural Landscape,* Lambert Academic Publishing: London.

12   Builth, H. *Ancient Aboriginal Aquaculture Rediscovered: The archaeology of an Australian Cultural Landscape,* Lambert Academic Publishing: London.

13   McNiven, I. (2017) 'The detective work behind the Budj Bim eel traps World Heritage bid', *The Conversation,* 8 February, <theconversation. com/the-detective-work-behind-the-budj-bim-eel-traps-world-heritage-bid-71800>.

14   Marks, L. (2018) 'Did Aboriginal and Asian people trade before European settlement in Darwin?' ABC News, 15 May, <www.abc.net. au/news/2018-01-16/aboriginal-people-asians-trade-before-european-settlement-darwin/9320452>.

15   Hunter, B, & J. Carmody (2015) 'Estimating the Aboriginal Population in Early Colonial Australia: The Role of Chickenpox Reconsidered', *Australian Economic History Review,* 55(2): 112–138.

16   Hunter, B, & J. Carmody (2015) 'Estimating the Aboriginal Population in Early Colonial Australia: The Role of Chickenpox Reconsidered', *Australian Economic History Review,* 55(2): 112–138.

17   Hunter, B, & J. Carmody (2015) 'Estimating the Aboriginal Population in Early Colonial Australia: The Role of Chickenpox Reconsidered', *Australian Economic History Review,* 55(2): 112–138.

18   ABC (2018) *Sydney: first encounters,* Rear Vision, 28 January, <www.abc.net.au/radionational/programs/rearvision/sydney-first-encounters/9361056>.

19   Barta, T. (2008) 'Sorry, and not sorry, in Australia: How the apology to the stolen generations buried a history of genocide', *Journal of Genocide Research,* 10(2): 201–214.

20   Walsh, A. (2018) 'My childhood', in Heiss, A. (ed.) *Growing up Aboriginal in Australia,* Black Inc.: Carlton.

21   Walsh, A. (2018) 'My childhood', in Heiss, A. (ed.) *Growing up Aboriginal in Australia,* Black Inc.: Carlton.

22   Dudgeon, P., M. Wright, Y. Paradies, D. Garvey, and I. Walker (2010) The social, cultural and historical context of Aboriginal and Torres Strait Islander Australians. In Working together: Aboriginal and Torres Strait islander mental health and wellbeing principles and practice. Australian Institute of Health and Welfare, Canberra, pp. 25–42.

23   ABS, Australian Historical Population Statistics, 2016, Cat. No. 3105.0.65.001, Australian Bureau of Statistics, Canberra.

24   Gantor, R. (2006) *Mixed Relations: Asian-Aboriginal contact in North Australia,* University of Western Australia Press: Perth.

25   McDonald, P. (2014) 'Population: An ever-present policy issue', in A. McClelland & P. Smyth (eds.) *Social Policy in Australia: Understanding for Action.* Australia: Oxford University Press, pp. 127–142.

26 Macintyre, S. (1993) *The Oxford History of Australia, volume 4: The Succeeding Age 1901–1942*, Oxford University Press: South Melbourne.

27 McDonald, P. (2014) 'Population: An ever-present policy issue', in A. McClelland & P. Smyth (eds.) *Social Policy in Australia: Understanding for Action*. Australia: Oxford University Press, pp. 127–142.

28 Allen, L. (2017) 'Australia doesn't have a population policy – why?', *The Conversation*, 3 July, <theconversation.com/australia-doesnt-have-a-population-policy-why-78183>.

29 Bolton, G. (1996) *The Oxford History of Australia, volume 5: The Middle Way 1942–1995*, Oxford University Press: South Melbourne.

30 Bolton, G. (1996) *The Oxford History of Australia, volume 5: The Middle Way 1942–1995*, Oxford University Press: South Melbourne.

31 Jupp, J. (2011) 'Politics, Public Policy and Multiculturalism', in Clyne, M. and J. Jupp (eds) *Multiculturalism and integration : a harmonious relationship*, ANU Press: Canberra, pp. 41–52.

32 Bolton, G. (1996) *The Oxford History of Australia, volume 5: The Middle Way 1942–1995*, Oxford University Press: South Melbourne.

33 Macintyre, S. (2009) *A Concise History of Australia* (Third Edition), Cambridge University Press: Port Melbourne.

34 Megalogenis, G. (2016) 'Correspondence', *The Australian Dream Quarterly Essay*, 64.

35 Siedlecki, S., & D. Wyndham, (1990) *Populate and Perish: Australian women's fight for birth control*, Allen & Unwin: Sydney.

36 ABS (1954) *Year Book Australia, 1954*, Cat. No. 1301.0, Australian Bureau of Statistics, Canberra.

37 McGuinness, P. (2018) *The Year Everything Changed: 2001*, Penguin Random House: Sydney.

38 Walker, K. (1966) *The Dawn is At Hand*, The Jacaranda Press: Brisbane, p. 9.

39 Bolton, G. (1996) *The Oxford History of Australia, volume 5: The Middle Way 1942–1995*, Oxford University Press: South Melbourne.

40 AIHW (2019) *Indigenous community safety*, Australian Institute of Health and Welfare: Canberra, <www.aihw.gov.au/reports/australias-welfare/indigenous-community-safety>.

41 Allen, L. (2018) 'I've overcome extreme disadvantage. For Australia to ever be equal, we must learn from stories like mine', *ABC News*, 26 October, <www.abc.net.au/news/2018-10-26/liz-allen-top-5-overcoming-extreme-disadvantage/10337006>.

Chapter 2 – From the cradle to the grave

1 Weisenthal, J. (2013). 'We love what Warren Buffett says about life, luck, and winning the "ovarian lottery"', *Business Insider*, 10 December,

<www.businessinsider.com/warren-buffett-on-the-ovarian-lottery-2013-12/?r=AU&IR=T>.

2   Wilkins, R., I. Laß, P. Butterworth and E. Vera-Toscano (2019). *The Household, Income and Labour Dynamics in Australia Survey: Selected Findings from Waves 1 to 17*. Melbourne Institute: Applied Economic & Social Research, University of Melbourne.

3   Allison, D. B., Kaprio, J., Korkeila, M., Koskenvuo, M., Neale, M. C., & Hayakawa, K. (1996). 'The heritability of body mass index among an international sample of monozygotic twins reared apart', *International Journal of Obesity*, 20(6), 501–506.

4   Skolnik, R. (2008). *Essentials of Global Health*, Jones & Bartlett Learning: Sudbury.

5   Allen, L. (2017). 'Politicians, stop pitching to the "average" Australian; being middle class depends on where you live', *The Conversation*, 11 December, <theconversation.com/politicians-stop-pitching-to-the-average-australian-being-middle-class-depends-on-where-you-live-88470>; Sheppard, J. and Biddle, N. (2017). 'Class, capital, and identity in Australian society', *Australian Journal of Political Science*, pp. 500–516.

6   Bronfenbrenner, U. (1994). Ecological models of human development International Encyclopedia of Education (2nd edition, Vol. 2). Oxford: Elsevier.

7   Bronfenbrenner, U. (1979). *The Ecology of Human Development: Experiments by Nature and Design*. Cambridge: Harvard University Press.

8   Bronfenbrenner, U. (1994). Ecological models of human development International Encyclopedia of Education (2nd edition, Vol. 2). Oxford: Elsevier.

9   Bronfenbrenner, U. (1979). *The Ecology of Human Development: Experiments by Nature and Design*. Cambridge: Harvard University Press, p. 3.

10   Bronfenbrenner, U. (1979). *The Ecology of Human Development: Experiments by Nature and Design*. Cambridge: Harvard University Press; Wise, S. (2003) *Family structure, child outcomes and environmental mediators: an overview of the Development in Diverse Families study* (Research Paper No. 30). Melbourne: Australian Institute of Family Studies.

11   Zubrick, S., Williams, A., Silburn, S., and Vimpani, G. (2000). Indicators of Social and Family Functioning: Department of Family and Community Services.

12   Kirk, D. (1996). 'Demographic transition theory'. *Population Studies*, 1996(50), 361–387; Omran, A. R. (1971). 'The epidemiologic transition:

A theory of the epidemiology of population change'. *The Milbank Memorial Fund Quarterly*, 49(4), 509–538; Omran, A. R. (2005). 'The epidemiologic transition: A theory of the epidemiology of population change'. *The Milbank Quarterly*, 83(4), 731–757.

13   Yaukey, D., Anderton, D., & Lundquist, J. (2007). *Demography: The Study of Human Population* (Third Edition). Illinois: Waveland Press, Inc.

14   Yaukey, D., Anderton, D., & Lundquist, J. (2007). *Demography: The Study of Human Population* (Third Edition). Illinois: Waveland Press, Inc.

15   Omran, A. R. (2005). The epidemiologic transition: A theory of the epidemiology of population change. *The Milbank Quarterly*, 83(4), 731–757; Yaukey, D., Anderton, D., & Lundquist, J. (2007). *Demography: The Study of Human Population* (Third Edition). Illinois: Waveland Press, Inc.

16   Yaukey, D., Anderton, D., & Lundquist, J. (2007). *Demography: The Study of Human Population* (Third Edition). Illinois: Waveland Press, Inc

17   Myrskyla, M., Kohler, H. & Billari, F. (2009) 'Advances in development reverse fertility declines', *Nature*, 460(7256): 741–743.

18   Johnstone, K. (2011) *Indigenous Fertility in The Northern Territory of Australia: Stalled Demographic Transition?* doctoral thesis, Australian National University.

19   Omran, A. R. (1971). The epidemiologic transition: A theory of the epidemiology of population change. The Milbank Memorial Fund Quarterly, 49(4), 509–538.

20   Olshansky, S. J., & Ault, A. B. (1986). The fourth stage of the epidemiologic transition: The age of delayed degenerative diseases. *The Milbank Quarterly*, 64(3), 355–391.

21   Gaziano, J. M. (2010). Fifth phase of the epidemiologic transition. *Journal of the American Medical Association*, 303(3), 275–276.

22   Popkin, B. M. (1994). The nutrition transition in low-income countries: An emerging crisis. *Nutrition Reviews*, 52(9), 285–298.

23   ABS (2019) *Australian Historical Population Statistics, 2016,* Cat. No. 3105.0.65.001, Australian Bureau of Statistics, Canberra; ABS (2019) *Australian Demographic Statistics, Dec 2018,* Cat. No. 3101.0, Australian Bureau of Statistics, Canberra.

24   ABS (2019) *Migration, Australia, 2017–18,* Cat. No. 3412.0, Australian Bureau of Statistics, Canberra.

25   ABS (2019) *Census of Population and Housing: Reflecting Australia – Stories from the Census, 2016,* Cat. No. 2071.0, Australian Bureau of Statistics, Canberra.

26   ABS (2019) *Census of Population and Housing: Reflecting Australia –*

Stories from the Census, 2016, Cat. No. 2071.0, Australian Bureau of Statistics, Canberra.

27   ABS (2019) *Australian Historical Population Statistics, 2016,* Cat. No. 3105.0.65.001, Australian Bureau of Statistics, Canberra; ABS (2018) *Births, Australia, 2017,* Cat. No. 3301.0, Australian Bureau of Statistics, Canberra.

28   Parr, N. and R. Guest (2011) 'The contribution of increases in family benefits to Australia's early 21st-century fertility increase: An empirical analysis', *Demographic Research,* 26(6): 215–244.

29   ABC, (2007) 'Costello takes credit for baby boom', *PM,* 27 June, Australian Broadcasting Corporation, <www.abc.net.au/pm/content/2007/s1963979.htm>.

30   ABS (2019) *Australian Historical Population Statistics, 2016,* Cat. No. 3105.0.65.001, Australian Bureau of Statistics, Canberra; ABS (2018) *Births, Australia, 2017,* Cat. No. 3301.0, Australian Bureau of Statistics, Canberra.

31   Melbourne Institute, *HILDA Statistical Reports,* <melbourneinstitute.unimelb.edu.au/hilda/publications/hilda-statistical-reports>.

32   Johnstone, K. (2011) *Indigenous Fertility in the Northern Territory of Australia: Stalled Demographic Transition?* doctoral thesis, Australian National University.

33   ABS (2018) *Births, Australia, 2017*, Cat. No. 3301.0, Australian Bureau of Statistics, Canberra.

34   ABS (2019) *Australian Historical Population Statistics, 2016,* Cat. No. 3105.0.65.001, Australian Bureau of Statistics, Canberra; ABS (2018) *Births, Australia, 2017,* Cat. No. 3301.0, Australian Bureau of Statistics, Canberra.

35   ABS (2019) *Australian Historical Population Statistics, 2016,* Cat. No. 3105.0.65.001, Australian Bureau of Statistics, Canberra.

36   ABS (2018) *Life Expectancy, States, Territories and Australia, 2015–17,* Cat. No. 3302.0.55.001, Australian Bureau of Statistics, Canberra.

37   AIHW (2017) *Trends in Indigenous mortality and life expectancy, 2001–2015: Evidence from the Enhanced Mortality Database.* Cat. No. IHW 174. Australian Institute of Health and Welfare, Canberra.

38   ABS (2018) *Deaths, Australia, 2017,* Cat. No. 3302.0, Australian Bureau of Statistics, Canberra.

39   Chao, F., P. Gerland, A. Cook, and L. Alkema (2019) 'Systematic assessment of the sex ratio at birth for all countries and estimation of national imbalances and regional reference levels', *PNAS,* 116(10): 9303-9311.

40   World Bank, (2019) *Sex ratio at birth (males births per females births),* <data.worldbank.org>.

41   Assari, S. (2017) 'If men are favored in our society, why do they die
      younger than women?', *The Conversation*, 9 March. <theconversation.
      com/if-men-are-favored-in-our-society-why-do-they-die-younger-than-
      women-71527>.

Chapter 3 – Modern demography

1   Mackellar, D. (2016) *My Country*, <www.dorotheamackellar.com.au/
      archive/mycountry.htm>.

2   ABS (2019) *Australian Demographic Statistics, Dec 2018*, Cat.
      No. 3101.0, Australian Bureau of Statistics, Canberra.

3   ABS (2019) *Regional Population Growth, Australia, 2017–18*, Cat.
      No. 3218.0, Australian Bureau of Statistics, Canberra.

4   ABS (2019) *Regional Population Growth, Australia, 2017–18*, Cat.
      No. 3218.0, Australian Bureau of Statistics, Canberra.

5   Dumont, G. (2018) 'Urban demographic transition', *Urban
      Development Issues*, 56: 13–25.

6   Hicks, N. (1978), *'This sin and scandal': Australia's population debate
      1891–1911*. Australian National University, Canberra, p. 23.

7   ABS (2018) *Australian Demographic Statistics, Jun 2018*, Cat.
      No. 3101.0, Australian Bureau of Statistics, Canberra; ABS (2019)
      Australian Historical Population Statistics, 2016, Cat. No. 3105.0.65.001,
      Australian Bureau of Statistics, Canberra; ABS (2018) *Population
      Projections, Australia, 2017 (base) – 2066*, Cat. No. 3222.0, Australian
      Bureau of Statistics, Canberra.

8   McDonald, P. and R. Kippen (1999) 'Population Futures for Australia:
      the Policy Alternatives', *Parliamentary Library* research paper 5
      1999–2000.

9   ABS (2018) *Australian Demographic Statistics, Jun 2018*, Cat.
      No. 3101.0, Australian Bureau of Statistics, Canberra; ABS (2019)
      Australian Historical Population Statistics, 2016, Cat. No. 3105.0.65.001,
      Australian Bureau of Statistics, Canberra; ABS (2018) *Population
      Projections, Australia, 2017 (base) – 2066*, Cat. No. 3222.0, Australian
      Bureau of Statistics, Canberra.

10   Olshansky, S.J,. D.J. Passaro, R.C. Hershow, et al (2005) 'A Potential
      Decline in Life Expectancy in the United States in the 21st Century',
      The New England Journal of Medicine, 352:1138–1145.

11   Dorling, D. (2019) 'Austerity bites – falling life expectancy in the UK',
      The BMJ Opinion, March 19.

12   Weeks, J. (2015) *Population: An Introduction to Concepts and Issues*,
      12th edition, Cengage: Boston.

13   Bongaarts, J. (2006) 'How long will we live?', *Population and
      Development Review*, 32(4): 605–628.

14 Productivity Commission (2013), *An Ageing Australia: Preparing for the Future*, Commission Research Paper Overview, Canberra.

15 Department of Treasury (2015), *2015 Intergenerational Report Australia in 2055*, Commonwealth of Australia, Canberra.

16 AIHW (2014) *Australia's health 2014*. Australia's health series no. 14. Cat. no. AUS 178, Australian Institute of Health and Welfare, Canberra.

17 ABS (2017) *Census of Population and Housing: Reflecting Australia – Stories from the Census, 2016*, Cat. No. 2071.0, Australian Bureau of Statistics, Canberra.

18 ABS (2019) *Migration, Australia, 2017–18,* Cat. No. 3412.0, Australian Bureau of Statistics, Canberra.

19 Housing, Income and Labour Dynamics in Australia Survey data 2016, wealth modules.

20 Housing, Income and Labour Dynamics in Australia Survey data 2016, wealth modules.

21 Housing, Income and Labour Dynamics in Australia Survey data 2016, wealth modules.

22 North, M. (2019) The Bank Of Mum and Dad Goes Boom!, Digital Finance Analytics Blog, 24 March, <digitalfinanceanalytics.com/blog/the-bank-of-mum-and-dad-goes-boom>.

Chapter 4 – Population panic

1 Allen, L. (2018) 'FactCheck: is Australia's population the 'highest-growing in the world'?', *The Conversation*, 13 July, <theconversation.com/factcheck-is-australias-population-the-highest-growing-in-the-world-96523>.

2 Allen, L. (2017) 'FactCheck Q&A: The facts on birth rates for Muslim couples and non-Muslim couples in Australia', *The Conversation*, 24 July, <theconversation.com/factcheck-qanda-the-facts-on-birth-rates-for-muslim-couples-and-non-muslim-couples-in-australia-81183>.

3 Karp, P. (2018) 'Australian senator who called for "final solution" to immigration expelled from party', *The Guardian*, 25 October, <https://www.theguardian.com/australia-news/2018/oct/25/australian-senator-who-called-for-final-solution-to-immigration-expelled-from-party>.

4 McCulloch, D. (2018) 'Senate sinks Anning's "White Australia" plebiscite', *The New Daily*, 18 October, <thenewdaily.com.au/news/national/2018/10/18/senate-sinks-white-australia-plebiscite/>.

5 'Fraser Anning punches teen after being egged while speaking to media in Melbourne', *ABC News*, 17 March 2019, <www.abc.net.au/

news/2019-03-16/fraser-anning-egged-in-melbourne-while-speaking-to-media/10908650>.

6   'Liberal candidate Kevin Baker quits race for Charlton over lewd
     website' (2013), *ABC News*, 21 August, <www.abc.net.au/news/2013-
     08-20/liberal-party-dump-charlton-candidate-kevin-baker-over-lewd-
     web/4900436.

7   Wilson, J. (2018) '"It's OK to be white" is not a joke, it's careless
     politicians helping the far right', *The Guardian,* 16 October, <www.
     theguardian.com/commentisfree/2018/oct/16/its-ok-to-be-white-is-not-
     a-joke-its-careless-politicians-helping-the-far-right>.

8   Shorten, B. (2018) *2018 Budget Reply Speech*, <www.billshorten.com.
     au/2018_budget_reply_canberra_thursday_10_may_2018>.

9   Lipson, D. and C. Gribbin (2017) 'Labor's "Australians First" ad sent to
     Bill Shorten's office before airing', *ABC News*, 9 May, <www.abc.net.
     au/news/2017-05-08/labors-australians-first-ad-sent-to-shortens-office-
     for-approval/8508660>.

10   Norton, A., Cherastidtham, I., and Mackey, W. (2019) 'Risks and
     rewards: When is vocational education a good alternative to higher
     education?' Grattan Institute.

11   McDonald, P. and J. Temple (2009) *Demographic and Labour Supply
     Futures for Australia*, Department of Immigration and Citizenship,
     Canberra.

12   Kainth, S. (2019) '13 years in Australia and I'm not a permanent
     resident yet', SBS, 2 October, <www.sbs.com.au/language/english/
     audio/13-years-in-australia-and-i-m-not-a-permanent-resident-yet>.

13   Infrastructure Australia, (2019) *An Assessment of Australia's Future
     Infrastructure Needs: The Australian Infrastructure Audit 2019*,
     Commonwealth Government, Canberra.

14   Razaghi, T., (2018) 'Sydney's infrastructure "still catching up after the
     city's 16 lost years": Federal Infrastructure and Cities Minister Paul
     Fletcher', *Domain*, 13 March, <www.domain.com.au/news/sydneys-
     infrastructure-still-catching-up-after-the-citys-16-lost-years-federal-
     infrastructure-and-cities-minister-paul-fletcher-20180313-h0xf5d/>.

15   Carr, B. (2009) 'Bob Carr Launches Mark O'Connor and Bill Lines'
     Overloading Australia', *People and Place*, 17(2): 81–85.

16   'NSW – the sad state' (2006) *The Sydney Morning Herald*, 28 July, <www.
     smh.com.au/national/nsw-the-sad-state-20060728-gdo21w.html>.

17   Department of Infrastructure and Transport (2011) *Our cities, our
     future: A national urban policy for a productive, sustainable and liveable
     future*, Commonwealth of Australia, Canberra.

18   ABS (2019) *Personal Income of Migrants, Australia, 2016-17*, Cat.
     No. 3418.0, Australian Bureau of Statistics, Canberra.

19   ABS (2019) *Australian Historical Population Statistics, 2016,* Cat.
      No. 3105.0.65.001, Australian Bureau of Statistics, Canberra; ABS
      (2019) *Australian Demographic Statistics, Dec 2018,* Cat. No. 3101.0,
      Australian Bureau of Statistics, Canberra.

20   ABS (2008) *Population Projections Australia, 2006 to 2101,*
      Cat. No. 3222.0, Australian Bureau of Statistics, Canberra.

21   Department of Treasury (2010) *Australia to 2050: Future challenges,*
      Commonwealth of Australia, Canberra.

22   Allen, L. (2011) 'Sustainable Population Strategy: Public Policy and
      Implementation Challenges, *The Academy of Social Sciences in Australia
      Proceedings,* 2/2011.

23   Allen, L. (2017) 'Australia doesn't have a population policy – why?',
      The Conversation, 3 July, <theconversation.com/australia-doesnt-have-
      a-population-policy-why-78183>.

24   Lowy Institute (2019) Lowy Institute Poll, <lowyinstitutepoll.
      lowyinstitute.org/themes/immigration-and-refugees>.

25   Lowy Institute (2019) Lowy Institute Poll, <lowyinstitutepoll.
      lowyinstitute.org/themes/immigration-and-refugees>.

26   Workman, A. and L. Sainty (2017) 'The Typical Australian Politician
      Is A 51-Year-Old White Man Who Owns Two Homes', Buzzfeed,
      12 April. <www.buzzfeed.com/aliceworkman/meet-andrew>.

27   Lowy Institute (2019) Lowy Institute Poll, <lowyinstitutepoll.
      lowyinstitute.org/themes/immigration-and-refugees>.

28   Home Affairs (2019) *Visa Statistics,* Department of Home Affairs,
      Canberra.

29   Koziol, M. (2019) '"This is a sham": Chaotic scenes as man ejected
      from Tim Wilson's franking credits inquiry', *Sydney Morning Herald,*
      8 February, <www.smh.com.au/politics/federal/this-is-a-sham-chaotic-
      scenes-as-man-ejected-from-tim-wilson-s-franking-credits-inquiry-
      20190208-p50wil.html>.

30   AEC (2019) *Elector count by division, age group and gender,* Australian
      Electoral Commission, Canberra.

31   Farrer, M. (2019) 'Tim Wilson's franking credits roadshow gets elderly
      audience fired up', *The Guardian,* 9 February, <www.theguardian.com/
      australia-news/2019/feb/09/tim-wilsons-franking-credits-roadshow-
      gets-elderly-audience-fired-up>.

32   'Fact check: Did abolishing negative gearing push up rents?' (2016),
      ABC News, 3 March, <www.abc.net.au/news/2015-05-06/hockey-
      negative-gearing/6431100>.

33   ABS (2018) *Census of Population and Housing: Estimating homelessness,
      2016,* Cat. No. 2049.0, Australian Bureau of Statistics, Canberra.

Chapter 5 – Demographic prospects

1 ABS (2018) *Population Projections, Australia, 2017 (base) – 2066*, Cat. No. 3222.0, Australian Bureau of Statistics, Canberra.

2 Coonan, C. (2019) 'Global population decline will hit China hard', *Deutsche Welle*, 9 September 2019, <www.dw.com/en/global-population-decline-will-hit-china-hard/a-50326522>.

3 ABS (2018) *Population Projections, Australia, 2017 (base) – 2066*, Cat. No. 3222.0, Australian Bureau of Statistics, Canberra.

4 Coonan, C. (2019) 'Global population decline will hit China hard', *Deutsche Welle*, 9 September 2019, <www.dw.com/en/global-population-decline-will-hit-china-hard/a-50326522>.

5 ABS (2018) *Population Projections, Australia, 2017 (base) – 2066*, Cat. No. 3222.0, Australian Bureau of Statistics, Canberra.

6 Shah, C. and Dixon, J. (2018), *Future job openings for new entrants by industry and occupation*, NCVER, Adelaide, p. 38.

7 ABS (2018) *Population Projections, Australia, 2017 (base) – 2066*, Cat. No. 3222.0, Australian Bureau of Statistics, Canberra.

8 ABS (2018) *Population Projections, Australia, 2017 (base) – 2066*, Cat. No. 3222.0, Australian Bureau of Statistics, Canberra.

9 ABS (2018) *Population Projections, Australia, 2017 (base) – 2066*, Cat. No. 3222.0, Australian Bureau of Statistics, Canberra.

10 ABS (2018) *Population Projections, Australia, 2017 (base) – 2066*, Cat. No. 3222.0, Australian Bureau of Statistics, Canberra.

11 'LNP senator says Australia's immigration policies like 'over stocking' paddocks', *SBS News*, 11 September 2019, <www.sbs.com.au/news/lnp-senator-says-australia-s-immigration-policies-like-over-stocking-paddocks>.

12 See, for example, the demography textbook: Weeks, J. (2015) *Population: An Introduction to Concepts and Issues*, 12th edition, Cengage: Boston.

13 See, for example, Diamond, J. (2005) *Collapse: How societies choose to fail or succeed*. Viking Press: New York.

14 Jarman, C. (2017) 'The truth about Easter Island: A sustainable society has been falsely blamed for its own demise', *The Conversation*, 13 October, <theconversation.com/the-truth-about-easter-island-a-sustainable-society-has-been-falsely-blamed-for-its-own-demise-85563>.

15 Visentin, L. (2019) '"They're my policies": Mark Latham's return from political wilderness', *Sydney Morning Herald*, 3 February, <www.smh.com.au/politics/nsw/they-re-my-policies-mark-latham-s-return-from-political-wilderness-20190201-p50v72.html>.

16 Smith, C. (2018) 'Premier calls for return to 'Howard era' immigration

levels', 2GB, 31 October, <www.2gb.com/premier-gladys-berejiklian-calls-for-return-to-howard-era-immigration-levels/>.

7 Bolger, R. and S. Awasthi (2019) 'Soaring temporary migrant numbers outstrip Morrison's "congestion busting" cut', *SBS News*, <www.sbs.com.au/news/audiotrack/soaring-temporary-migrant-numbers-outstrip-morrisons-congestion-busting-cut>.

8 ABS (2019) *Forward work program 2018-19*, Australian Bureau of Statistics, Canberra.

9 Martin, P. (2015) 'Abbott government considers axing the Australian census to save money', *Sydney Morning Herald*, 19 February, <www.smh.com.au/politics/federal/abbott-government-considers-axing-the-australian-census-to-save-money-20150218-13ieik.html>.

20 Cavill, A. (2014) 'Metadata laws introduced into parliament', *SBS News*, 30 October, <www.sbs.com.au/news/metadata-laws-introduced-into-parliament>.

21 Gal, U. (2017) 'The new data retention law seriously invades our privacy – and it's time we took action', *The Conversation*, 16 June, <theconversation.com/the-new-data-retention-law-seriously-invades-our-privacy-and-its-time-we-took-action-78991>.

22 'Census 2016: Reluctant senators to defy rules and leave names off survey', *SBS News*, 9 August 2019, <www.sbs.com.au/news/census-2016-reluctant-senators-to-defy-rules-and-leave-names-off-survey>.

23 Harding, S., Jackson Pulver, L., McDonald, P., Morrison, P., Trewin, D., Voss, A. (2017). Report on the quality of 2016 Census data, <www.abs.gov.au/websitedbs/d3310114.nsf/Home/Independent+Assurance+Panel>.

24 Brown, S. (2019) 'These menstrual tracking apps reportedly shared sensitive data with Facebook', *Cnet*, 10 September, <www.cnet.com/news/these-menstrual-tracking-apps-reportedly-shared-sensitive-data-with-facebook>.

25 Siedlecki, S., and D. Wyndham (1990) *Populate and Perish: Australian women's fight for birth control*, Allen & Unwin: Sydney, p. 6.

26 Thebaud, S., L. Ruppanner, S. Kornrich (2019) 'Men do see the mess – they just aren't judged for it the way women are', *The Conversation*, 2 July, <theconversation.com/men-do-see-the-mess-they-just-arent-judged-for-it-the-way-women-are-118728>.

Chapter 6 – Creating opportunities from challenges

1 Ellis, J., R. Mago, R. Kota, P. Dodds, H. McFadden, G. Lawrence, W. Spielmeyer, and E. Lagudah (2007) 'Wheat rust resistance research at CSIRO', *Australian Journal of Agricultural Research*, 58(6): 507–511.

2 Omran, A. R. (1971). 'The epidemiologic transition: A theory of the

epidemiology of population change'. *The Milbank Memorial Fund Quarterly*, 49(4), 509–538.

3   UNICEF (2019) 'This 'peanut butter' has changed the world: There's much more than meets the eye', *UNICEF in Action*, <www.unicef.org.au/blog/unicef-in-action/january-2019/this-peanut-butter-has-changed-the-world>.

4   Kirk, D. (1996). 'Demographic transition theory'. *Population Studies*, 1996(50), 361–387; Omran, A. R. (1971). 'The epidemiologic transition: A theory of the epidemiology of population change'. *The Milbank Memorial Fund Quarterly*, 49(4), 509–538; Omran, A. R. (2005). 'The epidemiologic transition: A theory of the epidemiology of population change'. *The Milbank Quarterly*, 83(4), 731–757.

5   Leavens, M. (2017) 'Do food miles really matter', *Harvard University Sustainability*, 7 March, <green.harvard.edu/news/do-food-miles-really-matter>.

6   Cook, J. D. Nuccitelli, S. Green, M. Richardson, B. Winkler, R. Painting, R. Way, P. Jacobs and A. Skuce (2013) 'Quantifying the consensus on anthropogenic global warming in the scientific literature', *Environmental Research Letters*, 8:2013.

7   Ulm, S., A. Williams, C. Turney and S. Lewis (2018) 'Australia's coastal living is at risk from sea level rise, but it's happened before', *The Conversation*, 16 January, <theconversation.com/australias-coastal-living-is-at-risk-from-sea-level-rise-but-its-happened-before-87686>.

8   See climate data for Penrith <www.bom.gov.au/climate/averages/tables/cw_067113.shtml> and Sydney <www.bom.gov.au/climate/averages/tables/cw_066062.shtml>.

9   'Australian heatwave: Canberra and Penrith smash temperature records that stood for 80 years', (2020) *The Guardian*, 4 Jan, <www.theguardian.com/australia-news/2020/jan/04/australian-weather-canberra-and-penrith-smash-temperature-records-that-stood-for-80-years>.

10   Longden, T. (2019) 'The impact of temperature on mortality across different climate zones', *Climate Change*, 157: 221–242.

11   Morris, L. (2017) 'Did you know Australia invented wi-fi?' *National Geographic*, 10 November, <www.nationalgeographic.com.au/australia/did-you-know-australia-invented-wi-fi.aspx>.

12   Alexander, R. (2020) 'How Are Immigration and Terrorism Related? An Analysis of Right- and Left-Wing Terrorism in Western Europe, 1980–2004', *Journal of Global Security Studies*, 5(1), 179–195, <https://doi.org/10.1093/jogss/ogy048>.

13   Doran, M. (2019) 'Tony Abbott warns West faces 'extinction' crisis, praises Hungary's far-right leader Viktor Orban', *ABC News*,

14 September, <www.abc.net.au/news/2019-09-14/tony-abbott-warns-extinction-crisis-viktor-orban-hungary/11513458>.

14   Allen, L. (2017) 'FactCheck Q&A: The facts on birth rates for Muslim couples and non-Muslim couples in Australia', *The Conversation*, 24 July, <theconversation.com/factcheck-qanda-the-facts-on-birth-rates-for-muslim-couples-and-non-muslim-couples-in-australia-81183>.

15   Cagle, S. (2019) "Bees, not refugees': The environmentalist roots of anti-immigrant bigotry', *The Guardian*, 16 August, <www.theguardian.com/environment/2019/aug/15/anti?CMP=share_btn_tw>.

16   Sherwood, S. (2019) 'Man accused of Christchurch mosque shootings pleads not guilty to 51 murder charges', *Stuff NZ*, 14 June, <www.stuff.co.nz/national/christchurch-shooting/113473357/terror-accused-pleads-not-guilty-to-murder-charges>.

17   Cagle, S. (2019) '"Bees, not refugees": The environmentalist roots of anti-immigrant bigotry', *The Guardian*, 16 August, <www.theguardian.com/environment/2019/aug/15/anti?CMP=share_btn_tw>.

18   'Gillard shuts door on "big Australia"', (2010), *ABC News*, 12 August, <www.abc.net.au/news/2010-06-27/gillard-shuts-door-on-big-australia/884050>.

19   Ware, H. (2016) 'Abbott's immigration policy: Open for business', *Social Alternatives*, 35(2): 48–55.

Conclusion – Demography needs a makeover

1   Australian Government (2019) *Planning for Australia's future population,* Canberra.

2   ALGA (2019) 'Commonwealth Treasury creates Centre for Population', *News and Events*, 12 July, Australian Local Government Association, Canberra.

3   Carey, G., P. McLoughlin and B. Crammond (2015) 'Implementing Joined-Up Government: Lessons from the Australian Social Inclusion Agenda', *Australian Journal of Public Administration*, 74(2):176–186, p. 176.

4   Carey, G., P. McLoughlin and B. Crammond (2016) 'Implementing Joined-Up Government: Lessons from the Australian Social Inclusion Agenda', *Australian Journal of Public Administration*, 74(2):176–186, p. 176.

5   Wilkins, R., I. Laß, P. Butterworth and E. Vera-Toscano (2019) *The Household, Income and Labour Dynamics in Australia Survey: Selected Findings from Waves 1 to 17.* Melbourne Institute: Applied Economic & Social Research, University of Melbourne.

Index

Index

Index

* 9 7 8 1 7 4 2 2 3 6 5 0 6 *